Cambridge Elements

Elements in Gene
edited
Robert Fro
Princeton Uni

COORDINATE STRUCTURES

Ning Zhang
National Chung Cheng University

CAMBRIDGE
UNIVERSITY PRESS

Shaftesbury Road, Cambridge CB2 8EA, United Kingdom

One Liberty Plaza, 20th Floor, New York, NY 10006, USA

477 Williamstown Road, Port Melbourne, VIC 3207, Australia

314–321, 3rd Floor, Plot 3, Splendor Forum, Jasola District Centre,
New Delhi – 110025, India

103 Penang Road, #05–06/07, Visioncrest Commercial, Singapore 238467

Cambridge University Press is part of Cambridge University Press & Assessment,
a department of the University of Cambridge.

We share the University's mission to contribute to society through the pursuit of
education, learning and research at the highest international levels of excellence.

www.cambridge.org
Information on this title: www.cambridge.org/9781009467926

DOI: 10.1017/9781009326643

First published 2023

A catalogue record for this publication is available from the British Library

ISBN 978-1-009-46792-6 Hardback
ISBN 978-1-009-32663-6 Paperback
ISSN 2635-0726 (online)
ISSN 2635-0718 (print)

Coordinate Structures

Elements in Generative Syntax

DOI: 10.1017/9781009326643
First published online: November 2023

Ning Zhang
National Chung Cheng University

Author for correspondence: Ning Zhang, zongningzhang@gmail.com

Abstract: In a coordination construction, which is universally available, two or more syntactic constituents are combined, with or without an overt coordinator. This Element examines how coordinate structures are derived syntactically, focussing on the syntactic operations involved, including constraints on both their operations and the representations they produce. Specifically, considering the recent research development in the syntax of coordination, the Element discusses whether any special syntactic operation is required to derive various coordinate constructions, including constructions in which each conjunct has a gap, whether there is any special functional category heading coordinate constructions in general, what the morphosyntactic statuses of coordinators (i.e., conjunctions and disjunctions) are in some specific languages, whether the structure of a coordinate construction can be beyond the binary complementation structure, and whether the mobility of conjuncts and the mobility of elements in conjuncts require any construction-specific constraint on syntactic operations.

Keywords: coordinate, J, modification, linker, category

ISBNs: 9781009467926 (HB), 9781009326636 (PB), 9781009326643 (OC)
ISSNs: 2635-0726 (online), 2635-0718 (print)

Contents

1 Introduction

A coordinate construction such as *water and fire* contains at least two conjuncts, such as the nouns *water* and *fire*, and an overt or null coordinator, such as the conjunction *and*, the disjunctive *or*, or the adversive joining marker *but*. This Element is about the syntactic relations between conjuncts, the ways to build the construction, and the morphosyntactic properties of the components of the construction: coordinators and conjuncts.

As has been found by many scholars in the literature, conjuncts are not structurally symmetrical. Major evidence for the asymmetry will be introduced in this Element.

Linguistic elements are divided into functional ones, such as the article *the* and the complementizer *that*, and lexical ones, such as nouns and verbs. Coordinators belong to the functional type. However, intuitively, we know that *water and fire* is just a nominal, and *read and write* is just a verbal expression. The available syntactic categories (called parts of speech in traditional grammar) cover all possible types of coordinate structures. Thus, coordinate structures do not represent an independent category, in contrast to other categories. This Element tells us how this intuition is captured in syntax.

This Element also shows that in a coordinate construction with two conjuncts, one conjunct is the complement of the coordinator, and the formed cluster must be merged with the other conjunct, and the whole coordinate complex is categorized by the latter conjunct. We thus see two basic levels of merger in forming a coordinate construction: complementation and categorization. The Element also reveals that the same two basic levels of merger also occur in constructions that have three or more conjuncts.

This Element further shows that the same two levels of merger are also found in a modification construction, where the structural position of a coordinator is that of a modification marker, which is visible in languages such as Mandarin Chinese but not in languages such as English. An overt or covert modification marker is merged with a modifier, and the formed cluster must be merged with the modified element, and the whole construction is categorized by the modified element. Thus, we achieve a new understanding of the relation between coordination and modification. It is the semantic relation between the linked elements and the properties of the element that realizes the relevant functional head that distinguish coordinate and modification readings of the two constructions.

In Section 2, the asymmetrical relation between conjuncts is discussed, and the parallel syntactic relation between a modifier and the modified element is also presented. In Section 3, the morphosyntactic properties of coordinators are explored, and a unified syntactic analysis of coordinators and modification markers is proposed. In Section 4, I show that building a coordinate construction is similar to building other kinds of complexes, and thus there is no coordinate construction-specific constraint on syntactic operations. In Section 5, certain (complex) coordinate constructions are derived. The derivations do not need any coordination-specific syntactic operations. Section 6 concludes the Element.

2 The Syntactic Relations between Conjuncts

In this section, the issue how conjuncts are integrated into a structure is addressed. I focus on the most basic construction, the one that has only two conjuncts, leaving larger coordinate constructions to Section 3. I argue that there are two levels of merger: complementation and categorization. The mergers are motivated by the properties of coordinators. Also, the same two levels of merger are seen in modification constructions.

One theoretical assumption of this Element is that syntactic merger is binary. See Yngve (1960: 453) and Collins (1997: 77; 2022), among others, for why this assumption is reasonable.

2.1 The Merger of a Coordinator and One of the Conjuncts

In this section, I argue for the functional element status of coordinators, showing how they take one conjunct as their complement.

Elements in syntactic structures can be lexical or functional. Typical lexical elements include n, v, and a. They can be either substantive or predicative. Lexical elements can function as the semantic core of a predicate or argument (subject or object), whereas functional ones cannot (Chomsky 2019: 52). A coordinator, such as *and* and *or*, is also neither substantive nor predicative. It exhibits the formal properties of functional elements, rather than those of lexical ones.

First of all, a coordinator has no theta relation with any other element in a structure. A theta relation identifies the role of an event participant (e.g., agent, theme, goal). If an element does not have such a relation with another element in a structure, it is a pure functional head. Pure functional elements include C and T. Similarly, a coordinator does not assign any theta role to a conjunct (or any other element). Therefore, it behaves like a pure functional element.

Secondly, a coordinator must be merged with conjuncts. A functional head must be merged with an element (e.g., T with a vP, or C with a TP), although it does not have a theta relation with the latter. Similarly, a coordinator must be merged with one conjunct first. The element that a head is merged with for the first time is the complement of the head (e.g., Chomsky 2002: 133–134).

In *water and fire*, for example, if *and* and *fire* are merged first, *fire* is the complement of *and*, but *water* is not. The latter is merged with in the next step, as shown in (1).

(1)

water

and^{HEAD}   fire^{COMPLEMENT}

This means that conjuncts are not structurally symmetrical: the one that is the complement of a coordinator is c-commanded by the other conjunct.

This asymmetry has long been recognized in the literature (e.g., Thiersch 1985; Munn 1987; Kayne 1994; Zoerner 1995). Binding facts show that the first conjunct can asymmetrically c-command the second one (Moltmann 1992). For instance, in (2a), the first conjunct *every man* can bind *his* in the second conjunct. However, in (2b), the second conjunct *every man* cannot bind *his* in the first conjunct. Thus, the two conjuncts are not structurally symmetrical.

(2)   a. Every man$_i$ and his$_i$ dog left.   b. *His$_i$ dog and every man$_i$ left.

This asymmetry does not come from the surface linear order (cf. Progovac 1998; Neeleman et al. 2023: 61). The contrast between (2a) and (2b) cannot be explained by the assumption that a quantifier can only bind a pronoun to its right. In examples like (3) (Culicover & Jackendoff 1997: 204), a quantifier binds a pronoun to its left. Also, see den Dikken (2018: 88) for more arguments against the precedence analysis of binding.

(3)   If you come up with a few more nice stories about him$_i$, every senator$_i$ will change his vote in your favor.

The asymmetry between conjuncts can also be seen in the relation between a referential expression (R-expression) and a pronoun. In (4a), the R-expression *John* in the first conjunct may be coreferential with the second conjunct, the pronoun *he*; but in (4b), where the order of the conjuncts is reversed, this coreferential relation disappears (Munn 1992). Since an R-expression cannot be c-commanded by a coreferential expression, the contrast in (4) again shows that the first conjunct asymmetrically c-commands the second one. See more similar asymmetries in Zhang (2010: 11–13).

(4)   a. John$_i$'s dog and he$_i$ went for a walk.   b. *He$_i$ and John$_i$'s dog went for a walk.

Licensing a negative polarity item (NPI) also shows a similar asymmetry. If the first conjunct is negative, it can license an NPI in the second conjunct, but not vice versa, as seen in the acceptability contrast in (5) and (6) (cf. Progovac 1998). Since the licensing needs an asymmetrical c-command relation, the contrast in these examples indicates that the first conjunct asymmetrically c-commands the second one.

(5)   a. No cat or any dog has entered this building.
         b. *Any cat or no dog has entered this building.

(6)   a. I met [no professors or anyone else]. (Hoeksema 2000: 124)
         b. *I met [any professors or no one else].

We thus see that in a coordinate construction, one of the conjuncts is syntactically lower than the other. This conjunct is the complement of the coordinator (also called internal conjunct).

The head element status of coordinators is also seen in the following point. In a head-complement cluster, the complement cannot decide the category of the cluster; similarly, the category of the internal conjunct is invisible. If the complement of a coordinator cannot satisfy the category-selection (henceforth c-selection) of a higher head, the construction can still be acceptable. In a coordinate construction in English, if the two conjuncts are of different categories, it is always the one that is next to X that satisfies the c-selection of X, and the category of the other conjunct does not have to. This has been discussed in Zhang (2010: 50–54) and confirmed by Bruening's (2022) experimental investigation. A preposition c-selects an NP, but not a declarative CP (Pesetsky 1991: 5), as seen in (7b).[1] In (7a), the first conjunct, which is an NP, but not the second one, which is a declarative clause, satisfies the c-selection of *on*. In (7c), the first conjunct, a CP, does not satisfy the c-selection of *on*, and the example is not acceptable. The examples in (8) and (9) show the same point.

(7)   a. You can depend on [NP my assistance] and [CP that he will be on time].
         b. *You can depend on [CP that he will be on time].
         c. *You can depend on [CP that he will be on time] and [NP my assistance].

(8)   a. We talked about Mr. Golson's many qualifications and that he had worked at the White House.
         b. *We talked about that he had worked at the White House.

(9)   a. Pat was annoyed by [the children's noise and that their parents did nothing to stop it].
         b. *Pat was annoyed by that their parents did nothing to stop it. (Sag et al. 1985: 165)

---

[1] A preposition can be followed by a WH-CP (e.g., *My happiness depends on whether you will talk to me or not*).

If one thinks that the CP in (7a) is headed by a null noun and thus the two conjuncts are both nominals (cf. Neeleman et al. 2023: §3.2), one still cannot explain why the assumed null noun cannot rescue other unacceptable examples in (7) through (9). Thus, there is indeed an asymmetry between the two conjuncts and changing the category would not predict it.

In addition to the selection of a preposition, the selection of a transitive verb also shows the categorial decisiveness of a single conjunct in English. The verb *devour* c-selects an NP, instead of any other category. In the acceptable (10a) (adapted from Grosu 1985: 232), the first conjunct *only pork* is an NP, satisfying the c-selection of the verb, and the second conjunct *only at home* can be either a PP, or a clause, such as *he did so only at home*, after the pre-PP part is deleted. In the unacceptable (10b), the first conjunct is either a PP or a clause with ellipsis and the second one is an NP. Neither a PP nor a clause can satisfy the c-selection of *devour*. The two conjuncts are categorially asymmetrical. The acceptability contrast between (10a) and (10b) indicates that it is the conjunct next to the verb that satisfies the c-selection of the verb.

(10) a. John devoured [NP only pork] and [PP only at home].
      b. ?*John devoured [PP only at home] and [NP only pork].

The above discussion shows that it is not true that "[a] coordination of α and β is admissible at a given place in sentence structure if and only if each of α and β is individually admissible at that place with the same function" (Huddleston and Pullum, 2006: 201; also see Przepiórkowski 2022a: 613 for a similar statement).

Note that our argument is based on the acceptable coordinate complexes whose two conjuncts have different categories (cf. Section 4.1.2). If a theory claims that conjuncts are symmetrical to each other (Blümel 1914: 193, 205; Bloomfield 1933: 185; Gleitman 1965: 276; 1965: 12–13, 196 n.7; Dik 1968; Jackendoff 1977: 51; Neeleman et al. 2023), either the a-forms in (7) through (10) should be unacceptable, or both the a-forms there and the version in (7c), (8c), (9c), and (10b) should be possible, contrary to fact.[2]

One might wonder if conjuncts are not symmetrical, why they seem to be permutable in examples like (11a) and (11b) (Blümel 2017: 129):

(11) a. Mary and Susi went to the cinema. b. Susi and Mary went to the cinema.

---

[2] Bruening & Al Khalaf (2020: (4)) mention the book title *The Once and Future King*, which is from the Latin *Rex quondam, Rexque futurus* 'Former King, and Future King.' Unlike *former*, *once* cannot modify a noun. Just like a contrastive modifier (e.g., *black and white* television), the modifier of *king* is [*once and future*]. Then, in the J-theory (Section 2.2 and Section 2.3), the structure of the modification expression is (i), where *once* is the complement of *and*, and thus it has no direct relation to *king*. Thus, the inability of *once* to modify the noun is not a problem.

(i)   [DP the [NP [J-set [J-set once and] future] king]]

My answer is that if merger is binary, each time only one element is combined with another element. It is possible for an early merged element and a later merged element to be semantically parallel. In (11a), *Susi* is merged with *and* first; and in (11b), *Mary* is merged with *and* first. But the syntactic structure of the coordination is still asymmetrical: The early merged one is lower than the later merged one, as shown in the binding, NPI-licensing, and c-selection facts.

Functional elements of the same type realize the same functional head in syntactic structures. For example, the finite complementizer *that*, the nonfinite complementizer *for*, and the complementizer *if* all realize the head C. I claim that various coordinators, including the conjunction *and*, the disjunction *or*, and the adversive joining marker *but*, realize a functional head position Junct (J). I call the combination of J and its complement J-set. This merger of a J element and its complement is the first step in building a coordinate construction. We discuss the next step in Section 2.2.

2.2 The Merger of a J-Set with the Other Conjunct

Why must a coordinate construction have more than one conjunct syntactically? In other words, why must a J-set be merged with another conjunct? In this section, I argue that J has no syntactic category, and it is this property that forces a J-set to be merged with another element, which is the higher conjunct.

Unlike any other phrase, a J-set cannot be used as an argument or predicate. It is well-known that a VP or AP can be a predicate and an NP can be either an argument or predicate. A PP can also be either an argument, as seen in (12a), or a predicate, as seen in (12b) and (12c) (Déchaine 2005). As shown in (13) and (14), a J-set can neither be an argument nor a predicate. Only the entire coordinate complex can be.

(12) a. Lucy put the brooms [$_{PP}$ against the door]]
  b. Smoking is [$_{PP}$ against the law]
  c. I consider [this [$_{PP}$ against human nature]]

(13) a. Lucy put the brooms [here and there]
  b. *Lucy put the brooms [$_{J\text{-set}}$ and there]]

(14) a. I consider [this [right and nice]]
  b. *I consider [this [$_{J\text{-set}}$ and nice]]

In order to explain the obligatory occurrence of a higher conjunct in addition to the one that is the complement of a coordinator, we need to distinguish the property of complement-taking (all functional heads have this property) and the property of carrying syntactic category features. I want to show that these two properties do not have to be bundled together.

Verbs have verbal categorial features, nouns have nominal categorial features, adjectives also have categorial features, and so on. Only an element that has category features can be c-selected by another element. In contrast, a root, which is among the building blocks of syntactic structures (Panagiotidis & Nóbrega 2023: 2), does not have category features. In generative grammar, when a root is merged with the functional head n, the result is n; when a root is merged with the functional head v, the result is v. The root *SLEEP* is categorized by n in *a good sleep*, and is categorized by v in *I will sleep*, as shown in (15a) and (15b), respectively (e.g., Marantz 1997). The functional heads n and v are categorizers of roots.

(15) a.   n   b.   v
         n   √SLEEP   v   √SLEEP

Different roots enable the same simplex syntactic structure to be associated with different concepts (Panagiotidis & Nóbrega 2023: 38). Thus, the existence of roots shows that there are elements that have no syntactic category features.

Roots not only have no category features, but also do not take complements (Panagiotidis & Nóbrega 2023: 21). On the other hand, some elements, for example, the noun *glass*, the adjective *round*, and adverbs in general, have category features but they do not take any complement. We thus see that having syntactic categorial features and taking a complement are different properties.

Many familiar functional elements not only introduce their complement into a structure, but also provide a category to the resultant combination. When a functional element projects a category, the category is contrastive to other categories (e.g., T is different from C, D, n, etc.).

In Section 2.1, we have seen that coordinators are functional elements, and thus they introduce another element into a structure, that is, they take a complement. I argued for the functional element status of coordinators without considering the issue whether they have syntactic category features. In the following, I introduce the fact that although coordinators (called J elements) share the complement-taking property with other functional elements, they also share properties with roots. Therefore, they are different from other functional elements.

First, like a root, J does not have a syntactic category. When a verb is merged with a nominal complement, the result is a verbal, rather than nominal, expression. It is the verbal head that decides the category of the combination. However, the occurrence of a coordinator in a coordinate construction cannot decide the category of the whole construction. A coordinate construction can be nominal, verbal, or adjectival, as seen in (16), where *and* does not play any role in deciding the category of the combination.

(16)   a. water and fire   b. I will read and write.   c. She is tall and thin.

Thus, neither a J-set nor the whole coordinate structure can be categorially decided by a coordinator. This is because J has no syntactic category features (also see Zoerner 1995: 19; de Vries 2005: 91), and thus a J-set is not categorized and has no label.[3]

Second, like a root, a J-set needs a categorizer. A root cannot appear without being categorized; it must be categorized by combining with a category-defining element (Embick & Noyer 2012: 296). Similarly, a J-set, which has no category, must be categorized. The highest conjunct (called external conjunct) is a categorizer. The fact that the category of a coordinate complex is identical to that of at least one conjunct is not deniable. As stated by Chomsky (2013: 46), if the whole coordinate construction is γ, and "if the coordinated expressions are APs, then γ is an AP, etc." In (7a), (8a), (9a), and (10a), it is the category of the first conjunct that categorizes the J-set, making the whole coordinate complex to satisfy the c-selection of the complex by a higher element (i.e., P in (7a), (8a), (9a), and V in (10a)). We thus claim that in such nominal coordinate structures, it is the first conjunct that categorizes the J-set. Therefore, the structure of *water and fire* is (17), where the first conjunct *water* categorizes the J-set. *Water* is an NP and thus the whole structure is an NP.[4]

(17)

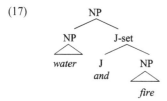

In all kinds of coordinate structures, the external conjunct, which may or may not be the first conjunct (see Section 2.3.5), categorizes a J-set.

---

[3] According to Chomsky (2013: 46), a coordinator cannot label a structure, but "it must still be visible for determining the structure." In Chomsky (2021: 33), "&" is treated like other atoms of computation such as INFL, but no elaboration on this "&" is seen.

[4] The two conjuncts in (ia) are of the same semantic type (<e,t>). Elements of this semantic type cannot occur in a subject position, as seen in (ib). If *a republican* in (ib) is interpreted as an individual, it then can neither be conjoined with the predicate-denoting *proud of it*, nor be modified by any AP to its right. Thus, the unacceptability of such an example does not affect the generalization that the category of the coordinate structure is identical to that of a single conjunct.

(i)   a. He is a republican and proud   b. *A republican and proud of it entered the
           of it.   building.

As I stated earlier, the major role of a functional element is to introduce another element into a structure. This role does not depend on whether the functional element has a categorial feature or not. In (17), *and* introduces *fire* into a structure. But since the complement cannot decide the category of the head-complement combination, and J itself has no categorial feature, the categoryless J-set must be categorized by another element. In (17), it is the conjunct *water* that does the job.

The requirement of a categorizer for a categoryless element explains why the combination of a coordinator and one conjunct must be merged with another conjunct in syntax.

Third, like a root, a J-set is not selected by any element. For a coordinate construction, the occurrence of the external conjunct satisfies the c-selection of the syntactic context (Section 2.1), and therefore, the occurrence of the J-set is not syntactically required. Zhang (2010: 61) points out "[n]o syntactic position is found to be taken by coordinate complexes exclusively. For example, verbs such as *compare* select plural nominals, and the selected element can be either a coordinate complex or a simplex plural nominal." For example, both *I compared John and Mary* and *I compared the two persons* are well formed. Thus, a J-set is syntactically optional. This optionality means a dependency asymmetry: to get integrated into a structure, a J-set must be merged with a categorizer, but no element selects for a J-set. If an element can be merged with a J-set, it can also be merged with a categorized element. This is like the situation of roots. No element needs a root, but a root must be integrated into a structure by a categorizer. It is the absence of a category feature in J that causes a J-set to be optional to a categorized element.

Note that if an additional coordinator (e.g., *either*) occurs, both conjuncts are focused (Section 3.2.2), and thus the obligatory occurrence of two conjuncts is associated with the lexical properties of the correlative coordinators, rather than the syntactic structure of a coordinate construction.

After presenting the three shared properties of roots and J elements, we still need to emphasize that roots are not functional elements but J elements are (Section 2.1).

The contrasts between J and other kinds of elements are summarized in (18).

(18)   Contrasts between J and other kinds of elements

	examples	Introducing a θ role	With category features
Pure functional	Infl, C, D, Num	−	+
	J	−	−
Semi-functional	Voice	+ (agent)	+
lexical	N, V, A	+	+
	Root	−	−

Root is not a syntactic category, and there is no RootP. For the same reason, J is not a syntactic category and there is no JP. The functional element status of J comes from the arguments presented in Section 2.1, rather than from any labelling capacity. The term *J element* is just a cover term for various conjunctive, disjunctive, and adversive joining markers (it is also for modification markers, to be discussed in Section 3.4). The term *J* is a convenient term to name the structural position that is realized by a J element, and the term *J-set* is a convenient name to call the combination of a coordinator and its complement, a categoryless cluster.

Since J must take a complement and be categorized by another element, the structure of a coordinate construction is built by two levels of merger: the merger of J and its complement, and the merger of a J-set and its categorizer. In the former merger, J is the head, while in the latter merger, J or the J-set is not the head. In neither merger, the two sisters are symmetrical to each other. The former merger is seen in the syntax of functional elements and the latter merger is seen in the syntax of roots. Therefore, neither operation is coordinate construction-specific.

This analysis of the relations between conjuncts is superior to other available analyses of the relation in the literature (including Moltmann 1992; Munn 1992, 1993; Zoerner 1995; Johannessen 1998; de Vries 2005; Chomsky 2013 and related work), which do not capture the categoryless property of coordinators.[5]

2.3 Structure Sharing of Coordinate and Modification Constructions

In this section, I argue that the same two levels of merger identified in coordinate constructions are also seen in modification constructions. I claim that a modifier is introduced by a J element, which is a modification marker. This marker is not overt in languages such as English. Then, the syntactic position of a modifier is the same as that of an internal conjunct, and the syntactic position of the modified element is the same as that of an external conjunct. I present five shared structural properties of the two constructions,

---

[5] In Chomsky (2013: 46), a coordinate construction is derived by three basic steps: the two conjuncts are merged, the resultant structure is merged with a coordinator, and finally, the first conjunct moves to the left of the coordinator, as illustrated in (i) (See Chomsky 2021: 33 for a more elaborated version). In (i), after the merger of *water* and *fire*, one of them must move out in order for β to be labeled. If *water* moves, β receives the label from *fire*. Now, since *and* and the construction it heads (i.e., α) are not available as a label, γ receives the label from *water*.

(i) $[_\gamma$ water $[_\alpha$ and $[_\beta$ <water> fire]

The proposed (17) is different from Chomsky's (i) in two major aspects: the two conjuncts show up in their base-positions and thus the level of the merger marked by β does not exist, and the categoryless α is identified as a J-set. In both analyses, one conjunct decides the label, and the sister of this conjunct, α in (i) or J-set in (17), is unable to label a structure.

and later in Section 3.4, I further present seven shared structural properties of coordinators and modification markers.

2.3.1 The Categorial Decisiveness of a Single Conjunct

In (7) through (10), we saw that in a coordinate construction, if the two conjuncts are different in their categories, the external conjunct alone can decide the category of the whole complex. The category of the internal conjunct can be ignored. Similarly, in a modification construction, it is the modified element that decides the category of the whole complex. The category of the modifier is ignored in the c-selection of the whole complex by a higher element. Modifiers are invisible to labelling algorithm (Safir 2022: 2), because they are comple-ment of a (silent) modification marker, which is also a J element. Therefore, in both a modification and a coordinate construction, one element alone satisfies the c-selection of the complex by a higher element. This element is the categor-izer of the J-set.

2.3.2 Syntactic Optionality

When an adjective modifies a noun and an adverb modifies a verb, they are syntactically optional. The combination of a coordinator and a conjunct is also syntactically optional (Section 2.2). For example, removing the modifier *tall* in (19a) and *and a girl* in (19b) does not affect the well-formedness of the constructions.

(19)   a.   I met a (tall) boy.   b.   I met a boy (and a girl).

   Thus, a J-set is syntactically optional, although it enriches the whole con-struction semantically.

2.3.3 Stackability

Both modifiers and conjuncts can be stacked, unlike arguments. The number of modifiers can be unlimited syntactically. In (20), other than *young, happy, diligent*, and *smart*, more can be added.

(20)   I met a young, happy, diligent, . . ., and smart boy.

   Conjuncts can also be stacked, as seen in the unbounded unstructured coord-ination construction (Chomsky 2013: 45), such as (21).

(21)   a. John is tall, happy, hungry, bored with TV, etc.
         b. I met someone young, happy, eager to go to college, tired of wasting
             time, . . .

In both (21a) and (21b), more conjuncts can be added, and thus the number of the conjuncts is "unbounded"; also, among the multiple conjuncts, no one is syntactically dependent on another, and thus they are "unstructured." We discuss such constructions in Section 3.3.1.

2.3.4 Alternation Possibilities between Conjuncts and Modifiers

A modifier may have a nonmodifier reading. Consider (22). Reading B of this example is synonymous with the coordinate construction (23) (Progovac 1999: 154).

(22)   I read his paper quickly.
         Reading A: 'I engaged in a quick reading of his paper.'
         Reading B: 'There is an event of reading of the paper by me, and the event was quick.'

(23)   I read his paper, **and** quickly.

(22) is ambiguous but (23) is not. Progovac (1999: 155) points out that this contrast shows that (23) does not come from any ellipsis in (22). According to her, (23) involves the interpretation of two eventualities: one event (i.e., my reading his paper) and one state (i.e., the event being quick), but (22) is under-specified: In addition to this two-eventuality reading, it can also mean that there is only one eventuality, the event of quick reading, and this event was not necessarily quick. On this latter reading (Reading A), (24a) and (24b) are not contradictory, but (25) is. A similar analysis of the ambiguity of *quickly* is seen in Parsons (1990: 46).

(24)   a. Even a quick reading of his paper took me three hours.
         b. Even reading his paper quickly took me three hours.

(25)   *Even reading his paper, and quickly, took me three hours.

(22) in Reading B and (23) "involve identical underlying structures" (Progovac 1999: 155; also see Bošković 2020a: 230). I propose that (26a) is the structure of (22) in Reading A, and (26b) is the structure of (22) in Reading B. The latter structure is shared with (23), where J is realized as *and* ((26b) is similar to Progovac's (69)). In this structure, the complement of J denotes a predication in which *quickly* is a predicate of a null event argument, *e*. This *e* is coindexed with the vP to its left. It is thus a null pronominal event argument.

(26)

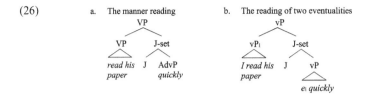

a. The manner reading

VP
├─ VP (*read his paper*)
└─ J-set
   ├─ J
   └─ AdvP (*quickly*)

b. The reading of two eventualities

vP
├─ vPᵢ (*I read his paper*)
└─ J-set
   ├─ J
   └─ vP
      └─ eᵢ *quickly*

A null pronominal event argument is also seen in the PRO in (27):

(27)   [The car collided with a lorry]ᵢ, PROᵢ killing both drivers. (Mittwoch 2005: 70)

Semantically, *quickly* in (26a) restricts the event kind denoted by *read his paper* into a sub-kind, while *quickly* in (26b) is a predicate of the event token denoted by *I read his paper* (cf. Gehrke & Castroviejo 2015). *Quickly* is a VP-modifier in (26a), but a predicate in an embedded predication in (26b). In (27), *killing both drivers* is a predicate of the event token denoted by the bracketed clause. In (26b), two vPs are conjoined, with an overt or covert coordinator at J.

Syntactically, the complement of J in (26b) can also be analyzed as a Small Clause, or Relator Phrase (RP) (see den Dikken 2006). In den Dikken (2006: 30–31), if a subject denotes an event, it can be the Specifier of an RP headed by -*ly*, and the complement of R, *quick* in (26b), moves to -*ly*.

In semantics, a modifier is conjunctive in general. Thus, the VP and the AdvP in (26a) undergo the semantic operation Predicate Modification (Heim and Kratzer 1998). In this sense, (26a) is also conjunctive, between two predicatives, VP and the adverb. But in (26b), the conjunctive relation is between two predication-denoting expressions (two vPs), and the adverb itself does not have a conjunctive reading.[6]

Moreover, an adverbial clause introduced by the temporal use of the complementizer *while* can get a conjunctive reading in examples like (28b) and (29b), similar to the coordinate constructions in (28a) and (29a), respectively (Haegeman 2022: 5).

(28)   a. John is doing a Ph.D. in Oxford but Bill did his first degree in Cambridge.
        b. John is doing a Ph.D. in Oxford while Bill did his first degree in Cambridge.

---

[6] One anonymous reviewer suggests that in both readings of (22), *quickly* is a modifier, and its position is low in the manner reading, but high in the other reading. A parallel height contrast should be seen in the restitutive and repetitive readings of *again*. In this alternative approach, if the unique reading of (23) is recognized, *quickly* is high exclusively, and no e argument occurs in (26b). The two approaches might be compatible with each other. They both show that the modification construction in (22) in one of its readings and the coordinate construction in (23) can be unified.

(29)   a. John reads the *Guardian* and Mary reads the *Times*.
        b. John reads the *Guardian* while Mary reads the *Times*.

A nonrestrictive modifier can also be analyzed as a conjunct to the modified element. De Vries (2005: 101) calls such a modification "specifying coordination."

On the other hand, a conjunct may have a modifier reading. The left conjunct in (30) has a conditional adverbial reading, and the right conjunct in (31a) has a purposive adverbial reading, similar to the infinitival adverbial in (31b). (30) and (31a) belong to the so-called "asymmetrical coordination" (AC).[7] See Freidin (2020: 48ff.) for more examples.

(30)   You drink one more can of beer **and** I'm   (Culicover & Jackendoff 1997)
        leaving.
        (= **If** you drink another can of beer, I'm leaving.)

(31)   a. Here's the whisky which$_i$ I [[went to the store] and   (Ross 1967: 168)
            [bought t$_1$]].
        b. Here's the whisky which$_i$ I [[went to the store] [to buy t$_1$]].

ACs and possible conjunctive readings of adverbials show that there is no absolute contrast between a conjunct and an adverbial in certain cases. They both can be the complement of J.

If an apparent modifier plays the role of a conjunct, as in (22) with Reading B, it has been claimed that "a silent conjunction" occurs (Progovac 1999: 156; also, Bošković 2020a: 230); if an apparent conjunct plays the role of a modifier, as in ACs, *and* does not function as a conjunctive coordinator. In some other constructions (e.g., heterofunctional coordinations (HFCs) and interwoven dependency constructions (IDCs) in Section 5), *and* is identified as an expletive coordinator. In all of these cases, the assumed silent or expletive conjunction realizes J.

In the analysis proposed here, both modification and coordination are represented by J in syntax. The reading alternation between a coordinate and modification construction is subject to semantic conditions. If both XP and YP denote a property, they have an intersective relation and undergo a Predicate Modification operation in semantics (Heim & Kratzer 1998). In this case, J can be realized by a (covert) conjunctive coordinator or modification marker. But if two entity-denoting nominals are conjoined (e.g., *the apple and the orange*), Predicate Modification does not apply, and thus no modification reading is possible. Our unified J account explains why the reading alternation is

---

[7] The term asymmetrical coordination is used in a semantic sense. Such coordination is also called "fake coordination" in the literature. Syntactically speaking, all conjuncts are syntactically asymmetrical.

possible, but it is up to semantics to explain where such an alternation cannot occur.[8]

2.3.5 The Position Flexibility of the J-Set

In principle, a modifier can either follow or precede its modified expression, as seen in (32a) and (32b), respectively. If a modifier is contained in a J-set, such examples show that a J-set can follow or precede its categorizer in modification constructions.

(32)   a.   I opened the door <u>quickly</u>.   b.   I <u>quickly</u> opened the door.

(33)   a.

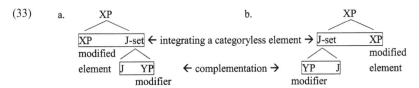

In Section 2.1, we introduced the relations between two conjuncts of a nominal coordination, with respect to binding, licensing NPIs, and the c-selection by a higher element, showing that the first conjunct asymmetrically c-commands the second one. The structure is thus similar to that in (33a). In this structure, a left conjunct cannot be a pronoun taking an element in the right conjunct as its antecedent (i.e., backward pronominalization), as shown in (34).

(34)   a.   John$_i$'s dog and {he$_i$/him$_i$} went for a walk.
         b.   *{He/him$_i$} and John$_i$'s dog went for a walk.

As for clausal coordination, we find two patterns: A, the left conjunct has an adverbial reading, and B, the elsewhere situation. Consider the pronominalization between α and β in a clausal coordination.

(35)   [... α ...] *and* [... β ...]

In Pattern A, backward pronominalization from the right clause is possible (Culicover & Jackendoff 1997; Privoznov 2021), as in a left adverbial construction. Some of the following data are from Privoznov (2021: 201–202) and the references therein.

---

[8] One anonymous reviewer asked me to clarify the relation between the integration of a J-set and the semantic operation Predicate Modification. If the integrator of a J-set and the complement of J both denote a property, the integration is Predicate Modification. Otherwise, it is not (e.g., if they denote propositions or entities).

The left-clause has a conditional reading:

(36) a. [Give it$_1$ fresh fish], and [a cat$_1$ will love you forever]. |A|
      b. [A picture of him$_1$ in the newspaper] and [a politician$_1$ will have high name recognition]. |A|
      c. [If you give it$_1$ fresh fish], [a cat$_1$ will love you forever]. |Adv|

The left clause has a concessive reading:

(37) a. You can [give it$_1$ fresh meat every day], [and still not make a tiger$_1$ your friend]. |A|
      b. Even if you can [give it$_1$ fresh meat every day], [still don't make a tiger$_1$ your friend]. |Adv|

In Pattern |B|, backward pronominalization from the right clause is impossible. Note that, according to Culicover and Jackendoff (1997: 198), if the verb of the left conjunct is not in a simple present tense, the conjunct does not have a conditional reading. Thus, the left conjunct in (38a) and (39a) does not have a conditional reading.

(38) a. [Some woman$_1$ sat at a table] and [the host offered her$_1$ drinks]. |B|
      b. *[She$_1$ sat at a table] and [the host offered some woman$_1$ drinks]. |B|

(39) a. Penelope [cursed Peter$_i$ and slandered **him**$_i$] |B|
      b. *Penelope [cursed **him**$_i$ and slandered Peter$_i$] (Langacker 1969: 162) |B|

We see more similarities between a left conjunct that has a conditional reading and a left conditional adverbial in the examples in (40) through (43). Such a left-conjunct (Pattern A) contrasts with other kinds of left conjuncts (Pattern B), in various kinds of dependency. If a pronoun is associated with a quantified nominal, which is not referential, the binding relation is not that of coreference. In (40), we see a contrast in such a binding between Pattern A and Pattern B left conjuncts. Parallel contrasts are also seen in the NPI-licensing in (41), Right-Node-Raising (RNR) in (42), and gapping in (43).

Binding   (cf. Privoznov 2021: 203; Culicover & Jackendoff 1997)

(40) a. **If** you give **it**$_1$ fresh fish, [every cat$_1$, no matter how wild it is, will love you forever]. |Adv|
      b. Give **it**$_1$ fresh fish, **and** [every cat$_1$, no matter how wild it is, will love you forever]. |A|
      c. *You gave **it**$_i$ fresh fish **and** every cat$_1$ has been locked up. |B|

NPI   (von Fintel 2001: 132; Keshet & Medeiros 2019: 886)

(41) a. **If** you have had left <u>any</u> later, you would have missed the plane. [Adv]
      b. Kobayashi eats <u>even one</u> more hotdog **and** he's the new champion! [A]
      c. *Kobayashi eats <u>even one</u> more hotdog **and** he likes catsup too. [B]

RNR   (cf. Culicover & Jackendoff 1997: 198)

(42) a. *If Big Louie finds out about _, then Little Louie puts out a contract on,
          [that guy who stole some loot from the gang]. [Adv]
      b. *Big Louie finds out about _, **and** Little Louie puts out a contract on,
          [that guy who stole some loot from the gang]. [A]
      c. Big Louie found out about _, **and** Little Louie put out a contract on,
          [that guy who stole some loot from the gang]. [B]

Gapping   (Culicover & Jackendoff 1997: 199)

(43) a. *If Big Louie steals one more car radio, then Little Louie _ the [Adv]
          hubcaps.
      b. *Big Louie steals one more car radio **and** Little Louie _ the hubcaps. [A]
      c. Big Louie stole another car radio **and** Little Louie _ the hubcaps. [B]

We summarize the contrast between Pattern A and Pattern B left conjuncts, compared with left conditional adverbials, in (44).

(44)

	Backward pronominal-ization	Binding from the right clause	NPI licensing from the right clause	Allow RNR	Allow gapping
Conditional Adverbial	√	√	√	No	No
Pattern A left-conjunct	√	√	√	No	No
Pattern B left conjunct	No	No	No	√	√

The above observations suggest that left clausal conjuncts may have different structural positions. If a left conjunct has an adverbial reading, it shares formal properties with a left adverbial and thus may occur in the same structural position as a left adverbial, that is, it is in the J-set, as in (45b) and (46b); otherwise, it is the sister of a J-set, as in (46a). The availability of the two orders is similar to that of an adverbial construction: a J-set can be to the right or left of its categorizer, seen in (33).

(45) a. You drink one more can of beer and I'm leaving.
      b.

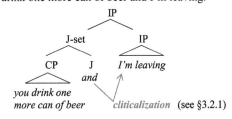

(46) a. XP   b.   XP

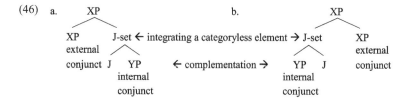

Position flexibility of a modifier is not found in all types of modification constructions. Also, the adverbial or modifier reading of a conjunct (Section 2.3.4) is not found in all types of coordination constructions. It is the possible existence of these phenomena that counts in our argumentation.

Importantly, we have seen that clausal coordination is different structurally from nominal coordination (Sections 2.1 and 2.2), a less studied issue. (34) shows that in a <u>nominal</u> coordination, backward pronominalization is impossible. But the <u>clausal</u> coordinations in (36) and (37) show that an element in the left conjunct can be a pronoun taking an element in the right conjunct as its antecedent if this conjunct has an adverbial reading, and thus backward pronominalization is possible. Elements of different categories surface at a similar position may have different syntactic positions. For example, nominal subjects and clausal subjects are syntactically different (Koster 1978; Lohndal 2014 and the references therein). It is thus not surprising to see that while the left conjunct is structurally higher than the right one in a nominal coordination (Section 2.2), it is lower than the right one, if it has an adverbial reading, in a clausal coordination.

Thus, in clausal coordination, we have distinguished the left-branching structure in (46b) from the right-branching one in (46a). We have seen that gapping and RNR are restricted to the right-branching one where J is realized by a coordinator, that is, a non-AC construction. In gapping, "both remnants of the gap are in a contrastive focus relationship to the parallel arguments in the first conjunct" (Johnson 2018: 595). This is possible only in a symmetrical coordinate construction, including an embedded one (e.g., *I saw some eat tomatoes on Tuesday and others apples*; Johnson 2018: 588; cf. Bošković 2020a: 238). Thus, not all coordinate constructions allow gapping and RNR.

2.4 Summary

In this section, I have argued that a coordinate complex is derived by two levels of merger: first, a conjunct is merged with a categoryless functional element J, and then, the result of the merger is merged with the other conjunct. The former merger is a normal complementation relation, and the latter one is a normal sisterhood between a categoryless element and its categorizer. Nothing is special in the syntactic computation. In this analysis, instead of specific syntactic categories (e.g. &, Boolean, Co) proposed in some studies (e.g. Zoerner 1995; Munn 1987; de Vries 2005), the coordinator J is recognized as a functional element. The distinction between the high (external) conjunct and the low (internal) one is attested in binding, NPI-licensing, and c-selection in a nominal coordination, and attested in whether the left conjunct exhibits systematic properties of left adverbials in a non-nominal coordination, with respect to pronominalization, binding, NPI-licensing, RNR, and gapping. Thus, not all types of left conjuncts occur in the same syntactic position: in a nominal coordination, the left conjunct is higher than the right one, but in a clausal coordination, the left conjunct is lower than the right one if it has a conditional reading.

Moreover, the analysis unifies the syntax of coordination and modification: both are derived by the two levels of merger mentioned earlier. The unification comes from the aspects of category, optionality, stackability, reading, and position. I will add one more fact to support this unification: the shared properties of coordinators and modification markers, in Section 3.4.[9]

Our two levels of merger for modification leads to a unification of operations to build modification constructions and nonmodification constructions (also see Safir 2022 for a similar unification from other perspectives). Also, not only a head element but also a phrase (phrasal conjunct or modified element) can be a categorizer.[10]

3 More about the Syntax of Coordinators

In the previous section, I have claimed that a coordinator realizes J, which is a functional head element without any categorial features. In this section, I show the possible c-selection of coordinators (Section 3.1), identify their linker position (Section 3.2), analyze their properties when more than two conjuncts occur (Section 3.3), and finally, present their shared syntactic properties with modification markers, to show that they both are J elements (Section 3.4). Thus, the functional head identified in the previous section is not coordination-specific.

---

[9] Trying to give a unified analysis of ATB gaps and parasitic gaps, Williams (1990) names an assumed function head COORD, to cover relevant syntactic relations. But his COORD is not a categoryless element and it also covers noncoordinate and nonmodification relations.

[10] Some scholars assume that roots are categorized by specialized functional heads such as n or v (e.g., Marantz 1997), but some other scholars assume that roots are categorized by their functional superstructure, without the need of a dedicated categorizing head (e.g., Borer 2005; Adger 2013). The categorization of a J-set is compatible with the latter theory.

3.1 Possible C-Selection of Coordinators

The availability of a category feature of X is different from the c-selection of X. C-selection is a category restriction of a head element on its complement, and it is lexical-specific. For example, *ask* selects for NP, as well as CP, but *inquire* selects for CP only (e.g., *John asked {the time/what time it was}; John inquired {*the time/what time it was}*). This difference has nothing to do with the verbal category of *ask* and *inquire*.

Like other functional elements, J introduces an element into a structure. This function is independent from the c-selection of the element that realizes J. The English coordinator *and* connects various categories (Section 4.1.1). However, as pointed out by Payne (1985: 5), the *and*-pattern of coordinators "is by no means universal." In many languages, different coordinators are used to coordinate conjuncts of different categories (e.g., Zhang 2010: 46–50 and the references therein). In Mandarin Chinese, the coordinator *gen* conjoins nominals, whereas the coordinator *you* cannot. The contrast is shown in (47).

(47)   a. Alan   xihuan   he   pijiu {gen/*you}   lü-cha.
            Alan   like   drink   beer and/and   green-tea
            'Alan likes to drink beer and green-tea.'
         b. Alan   shanliang {you/*gen}   youmo.
            Alan   kind   and/and   humorous
            'Alan is kind and humorous.'

The fact that coordinators such as *and* may occur in coordinate complexes of any category means that such coordinators do not c-select for any particular category. If a coordinator has any special requirement for the category of a conjunct, as shown in (47), the relation between the coordinator and the conjunct must be that between a head and its complement, since only head elements exhibit c-selection restrictions on their sisters. The c-selection restriction between coordinators and internal conjuncts thus provides an additional argument for the head element status of coordinators.

3.2 The Positions of Coordinators

3.2.1 Coordinators between Conjuncts: Linker

A coordinator generally occurs between the two conjuncts. How do we understand this position? When a morpho-syntactic dependency is established between two elements, the dependency relation can be marked by an overt form. Such an overt form can be morphologically attached to the dependent element or the other element, called Head (Nichols 1986) (note that the morphological Head can be different from the syntactic head in the generative syntax). For example, in Chechen, the initial consonant of the adjective shows its agreement with the covert gender class of the Head noun. In (48a), the prefix *d-* with the adjective *ovxa* 'hot' shows its agreement with the covert class d of the Head noun *xi* 'water' (the superscript ^{M} marks a dependent element, and the superscript ^{H} marks the Head element). This is a pattern of **dependent**-marking. In contrast, in (48b), the suffix *-i* with the Head noun *kůh* 'mountain' marks the noun as having a modifier, that is, the adjective *baland* 'high' in the Tadzhik example. This is a pattern of **Head**-marking (Nichols 1986: 61).

(48) a. ^{M}**d**-ovxa ^{H}xi   [Chechen] b. ^{H}kůh-^{M}**i** baland [Tadzhik]
          hot   water(d-)   mountain high
          'hot water'   'high mountain'

In addition to these two patterns of dependency marking, a third pattern is called **neutral** marking. In this pattern, a marker occurs between the two elements that have a dependency relation; importantly, the first element can be either the Head or the dependent. This pattern can be shown by the Tagalog examples in (49). In (49a), *nasa mesa* 'on the table' is a modifier, and *libro* 'book' is the modified Head; in (49b), the order is reversed; but in both cases, the linker *-ng* follows the first phrase (Nichols 1986: 65; L is for linker). A similar situation is seen in the Paiwan examples in (50) and (51) (Tang 2008).

(49) a. nasa mesa-^{M}**ng** ^{H}libro b. ^{H}libro^{M}-**ng** nasa mesa [Tagalog]
          on table-L   book   book-L   on table
          Both a and b: 'the book on the table'

(50) a. va'uan *(**a**) kun   b. kun *(**a**) va'uan   [Paiwan]
          new   L skirt   skirt L new
          Both: 'new skirt'

(51) a. [k-in-asengseng   ni   Kai]   *(**a**) kun
          make-PV   GEN   Kai   L   skirt
      b. kun *(**a**) [k-in-asengseng   ni   Kai]
          skirt   L make-PV   GEN   Kai
          Both: 'the skirt that is made by Kai'

When the neutral marking is seen in nominals, the marker is called a linker. But the pattern can also be seen beyond nominals. We can call a dependency marker of the neutral pattern a linker, regardless of the relevant categories of the expressions.

Moreover, a linker may have various forms depending on the formal context. Chung (1991: 97) introduces a linker in modification constructions in Chamorro and describes that "[w]hen the modifier precedes, the linker is realized as *na*; when the modifier follows, the linker is *-n* after a vowel and null otherwise." In (52a), the modifier precedes the modified noun, and in (52b), the modified noun precedes the modifier (Chung 1991: 97). Also see Pietraszko (2019) for linker form variations in other languages.

(52)   a. i Chapanis **na** lingguahi b. i lingguahi-**n** Chapanis [Chamorro]
            the Japanese L language   the language-L Japanese
            both a and b: 'the Japanese language'

Coordinators in languages such as English, Mandarin, and Japanese are also linkers, that is, they are dependency markers of the neutral marking type, which occur between two conjuncts, regardless of the structural hierarchy difference of the two conjuncts (Zoerner 1995: 11) (also see e.g., Dik 1983; Zwart 2005; Kayne 2022: 7).

If an element is a clitic, we need to identify not only its position in the whole construction, but also its position with respect to its phonological host, that is, whether it is a proclitic or enclitic. In English, a coordinator takes the conjunct to its right as its morphological host, whereas in Japanese, a coordinator takes the conjunct to its left as its morphological host (see Mitrović 2014: 27f. for enclitic coordinations in some other languages). (53) are examples of enclitic coordinators.

(53)   a. [Hanako-**to** Naoko]-wa   kawaii.   [Japanese]
            Hanako-and   Naoko-TOPIC pretty
            'Hanako and Naoko are pretty.'
        b. musuko-ga   sotugyoo   sita-**si**   musume-ga   yome-ni   itta.
            son-NOM   graduation did-and   daughter-NOM bride-DAT went
            'The son graduated and the daughter got married.'

Because of the two considerations (i.e., the neural pattern, which locates a marker between two elements that have a dependency relation, and the proclitic-enclitic contrast), the adjacency of a dependency marker with an element does not necessarily mean that they form a syntactic constituent, although a functional element forms a constituent with its complement. Thus, a coordinator, as a functional element, is grouped with one conjunct syntactically; but morphologically, it may be grouped with a different conjunct, as either a proclitic or enclitic, consistently. We have shown the cliticalization of *and* in (45b).

Also, since *and* is a proclitic, it disallows the conjunct to its right to be silent, as seen in (54b). In contrast, the conjunction *-to* in Japanese is an enclitic, and thus disallows the conjunct to its left to be silent, as seen in (55b).

(54)   a. Can linguists [study negation]? Not **e** and stay sane they can't.
        b. *Can linguists [stay sane]? Not study negation <u>and **e**</u> they can't.

(55)   a. A: Robin ate fish.   B: <u>And rice!</u>
        b. A: Robin-wa   sakana-o   tabeta. B: *<u>to gohan!</u> (Zoerner 1995: 33)
            Robin-TOP   fish-ACC   eat-PST   and rice

Linkers may occur in various syntactic contexts, not restricted to coordinate and modification constructions. The Tagalog example in (56) (Aldridge 2017: 9) shows a wide distribution of linkers in the language.

(56) ito=ng   dalawa=ng   mahaba=ng   libro   ni   Maria   [Tagalog]
      this.NOM=L   two=L   long=L   book   GEN   Maria
      'these two long books of Maria's'

A linker also occurs between a noun and its complement clause in Ndebele (Pietraszko 2019). This is also true of the formative *de* in Mandarin. Linkers occur in many languages, including Iranian languages and Balkan languages. Like clitic, linker is not a syntactic category. It is just a morphological pattern of dependency marking. It is not clear whether a linker has a consistent correlation with the nature of the dependency. It has been claimed that linkers may case-mark their complement (Larson & Yamakido 2008), head a phase (Richards 2010), close an extended projection (Philip 2012), head a DP-internal unsaturated category (Aldridge 2017), or rescue the illegal direct merger of elements that both bear visible φ-features (Shushurin 2022).

3.2.2 Null and Additional Coordinators in Binary Coordination

In addition to the Head-marking, dependent-marking, and neutral marking (i.e., by a linker), there are two more patterns of dependency marking. One is zero-marking (similar to the past tense marking on the English verb *cut*), on either the Head or the dependent. For example, neither the modifier *high* nor the modified *mountain* in *high mountain* has a dependency marker. In a coordinate construction, it is also possible that there is no overt coordinator (called asyndetic coordination or juxtaposition) (e.g., Haspelmath 2004), as shown in (57).

(57) a. I found no more than two, three mistakes in your article. (Neeleman et al. 2023: 74)
      b. They went, the one to Paris, the other to London.   (Kayne 1994: 144)
      c. Baoyu Daiyu,   ni   xihuan   na   yi-ge?   [Mandarin]
         Baoyu Daiyu   you   like   which   one-CL
         'Baoyu {and/or} Daiyu, which one do you like?'
      d. Qichuang-hou   dajia   dou   hui   shua   ya   xi   lian.
         get.up-after   everyone   all   will   brush   tooth   wash   face
         'After getting up, everyone will brush the teeth and wash the face.'
      e. Mei-jia   zhi   neng   lai   yi-ge   ren,   daren xiaohai   dou   xing.
         each-family   only can   come   one-CL   person   adult child   all   OK
         'Only one person from each family is allowed to come. Either an adult or a child is OK.'

The null coordinator can have a disjunctive reading in (57a) and (57c) and must have a disjunctive reading in (57e) (contra Winter 1994).

The last pattern is double marking, that is, a formal marking on both the Head and the dependent. One of Nichols's (1986: 72) examples is (58).

(58)   hwan-^{M}pa ^{H}hana-^{M}n-chaw   [Huallaga (Huánuco) Quechua]
        John-GEN   above-3-LOC
        'above John'

It is also possible for each conjunct to occur with a coordinator. In (59a), each conjunct is preceded by *et*; and in (59b), each conjunct is followed by *to* (Kayne 1994: 58).

(59)   a. Jean   connait   et   Paul   et   Michel.   [French]
           Jean   knows   and   Paul   and   Michel
           'Jean knows both Paul and Michel.'
        b. John-to   Mary-to-ga   kekkonsita.   [Japanese]
           John-and   Mary-and-NOM   married
           'Both John and Mary married.'

Moreover, in Latin, the conjunction *et* can alternate with the conjunction clitic -*que* in certain contexts (Carlson 1983; cf. Kayne 1994: 143 n. 3). The former always precedes a conjunct, and the latter follows the first prosodic word of a conjunct (e.g., Embick & Noyer 2001), as seen in (60). Conjunctions whose positions are similar to that of -*que* are also found in some other languages (Mitrović 2014: 73ff.).

(60)   a. senatus et   populus romanus   b. senatus   populus-que   romanus
           senate and people Roman   senate   people-and   Roman
           Both a and b: 'the senate and the Roman people'

Either *et* or –*que* can introduce a conjunct. The four possible combinations are all available:

(61)   a. et   Marcus   et   Julius   b. Marcus-que   Julius-que
           and   Marcus   and   Julius   Marcus-and   Julius-and
           Both a and b: 'Marcus and Julius'
        c. et   singuli   universis-que
           and   for.individuals for.all-and
           'both for individuals and for all together'   (Dik 1968: 44)
        d. dum   Augustus [seque   et   domum   et   pacem]   sustentavit
           while Augustus him-and   and   house   and   peace   upheld
           'as long as Augustus upheld himself, his house, and peace' (Dik 1968: 44)

For the same conjunct, either *et* or -*que* occurs, but never both. Thus, the two formatives are in complementary distribution with a conjunct, and they are different in their positions with respect to the conjunct. Like *-que*, the positions of certain coordinators in other languages, including Antient Greek, Sanskrit, Old Irish, West Greenlandic, are also decided by syntax-phonology interface conditions (e.g., *aber* 'but' in German). See Weisser (2020) and the references cited there.

Thus, in addition to one coordinator, an additional coordinator may occur in certain constructions. Additional coordinators have the following main properties. First, their occurrence depends on the occurrence of the other coordinator. They are thus repetitive and correlative elements (e.g., Zhang 2008b). Second, they mark the coordinate construction to be exclusively distributive (Kayne 1994: 146 n. 16; Progovac 1999, 2002; de Vries 2005; Zhang 2008b; among others), and thus such a construction cannot be the argument of a collective predicate, as seen in (62b).

(62)   a. Max et Léa forment un couple heureux. (Mouret 2004: (9))
           Max and Léa make a couple happy.
           'Max and Léa make a happy couple.'
        b. *Et Max et Léa forment un couple heureux.

Third, they are focus markers, instead of joining markers (e.g., Hendriks 2004; Zhang 2008b; Wu 2022) .

Johannessen (1998: 154) treats additional coordinators as adverbs. De Vries (2005: 91) points out that they should not be used to test the syntactic position of a coordinator (cf. Borsley 2005: 473–474; also see Wu 2022). For a real coordinator, as a J element, it is always syntactically grouped with its complement (i.e., the internal conjunct), although its morphological position may vary. In (61c), *-que* follows the first prosodic word of the second conjunct; and since this conjunct has one prosodic word only, *-que* appears at the right edge, for a morphological reason. This coordinator is a J element, but the left edge *et* is not, in this example. Cross-linguistically, no real coordinator is found at the left-edge of a coordinate complex (Haspelmath 2004: 6).

I conclude that in a minimal coordinate construction, which has two conjuncts, the distribution of the coordinator is like that of other kinds of dependency markers. A coordinator, as a J element syntactically, can be a linker morphologically, and thus, a syntax-phonology mismatch may occur in its surface position.

3.3 Coordinators in Non-minimal Coordinate Constructions

3.3.1 Syntagmatic Varieties of Coordinators

Coordinators can be conjunctive (e.g., *and*), disjunctive (e.g., *or*), and contrastive (e.g., *but*), semantically. Disjunctives can be further distinguished into inclusive (e.g., *or* in the absence of *either*) and exclusive (e.g., *yaoburan* 'or' in Mandarin). Conjunctives can be further distinguished into noncollective (e.g., *ji* 'and' in Mandarin; Zhang 2010: 128) and others. In this subsection, we introduce two less discussed types of coordinators: noniterative and nonexhaustive.

Some coordinators link two conjuncts only, e.g., *but* in English (Gleitman 1965: 266, 273), as seen in (63). *Danshi* 'but' in Mandarin behaves the same.

(63)   *John is ill but Mary isn't but Bill has a broken leg.   (van Oirsouw 1987: 7)

A coordinate complex with *but* is in the minimal form of coordination. There is no coordinator that must link exactly three conjuncts or exactly four (or any higher number) conjuncts (Zhang 2010: 70).

Moreover, in the presence of an additional coordinator (e.g., *both, either, neither*; see Section 3.2.2), a coordinator links two conjuncts only. In this case, the coordinator is used as a noniterative coordinator.

On the other hand, if the conjuncts denote elements of an open set, the coordinator is, or is used as, a nonexhaustive coordinator. Nonexhaustive coordinators can be found in many languages (Barotto & Mauri 2022), e.g., *ya* 'and' in Japanese (Zoerner 1995: 33 n. 8; 1999: 328 n. 7) and *a* 'and' in Mandarin (Zhang 2008a). The use of *a* in Mandarin is exemplified in (64a). Unlike other coordinators in the language, *a* is an enclitic, and thus it always follows a conjunct. In this language, such a coordinator can also be null, as seen in the synonymous (64b).

(64)   a. Zhuo-shang   you shu-a,   baozhi-a,   biji-ben-a, ...
            table-on   have book-and newspaper-and   note-book-and
         b. Zhuo-shang you shu, baozhi, biji-ben, ...
            Both a and b: 'There are books, newspapers, notebooks, . . . on the table.'
         c. [$_{NP}$ shu [$_{J\text{-set}}$ a [$_{NP}$ baozhi [$_{J\text{-set}}$ a [$_{NP}$ biji-ben [$_{J\text{-set}}$ a [$_{NP}$ *pro*]]]]]]]
                                                                                  cliticalization

In the J-theory, the structure of (64a) is (64c). The last coordinator *a*, as a J element, takes a radical *pro* as its complement, forming a J-set [*a-pro*]. This J-set is merged with its categorizer *biji-ben*, forming an NP [*biji-ben-a pro*]. Another *a* takes this NP as its complement, forming a higher J-set [*a-biji-ben-a pro*]. This J-set is merged with *baozhi*, forming another NP [*baozhi-a-biji-ben-a pro*]. One more *a* takes this NP as its complement, forming an even higher J-set [*a-baozhi-a-biji-ben-a pro*]. Finally, the NP *shu* integrates this highest J-set, forming the NP object of *you*.

But the lowest coordinate complex alone, whose second conjunct is a *pro*, is not acceptable, as seen in (65b), in contrast to (65a).

(65)   a. Zhuo-shang you baozhi-a, biji-ben-a, . . . b. *Zhuo-shang you biji-ben-a, . . .

This means that a nonexhaustive coordinator cannot occur in a minimal coordinate construction. It thus contrasts with a noniterative coordinator.

In English, nonexhaustive conjunctive coordinators are null consistently. They occur in the so-called unstructured coordination (Chomsky & Miller 1963; Chomsky 2013: 45), for example, the underlined part in (66a), compared to (66b). (66c) shows that an ATB version of such a construction is available.

(66)   a. I met someone <u>young, happy, eager to go to college, tired of wasting time, . . .</u>
       b. I met someone <u>young, happy, eager to go to college,</u> **and** <u>tired of wasting time.</u>
       c. Which musician does John have <u>pictures of, books about, records by, . . .</u> –
       you name it?   (Neeleman et al. 2023: 74)

According to Büring and Hartmann (2015: 44), an example like (66a) "gives an impression of incompleteness, a notion of the sentence still being 'up-in-the-air.'" So, in addition to the items mentioned, there may be more unmentioned items. We assume that in (66a), there are null versions of nonexhaustive coordinators. The structure of (66a) is similar to (64c).

Thus, the coordinate complex in (66a) is not "unstructured." Instead, the last conjunct can be a *pro*, and the whole construction is built via recursive applications of the two steps of merger as in other coordinate constructions: J-set forming and J-set categorization. In the construction, no conjunct is syntactically dependent on another, but since merger is binary, an early merged conjunct appears at a lower position than a later merged one. This is similar to the examples in (11).

In (67a) (Progovac 1998: 3), the occurrence of the word *etc* indicates the incompleteness of the conjuncts. The Latin word *etc* is the combination of *et* 'and' and *cetera* 'the rest.' The *et* part is J. The judgment of (67b) is not consistent. For those who reject it, *et* here is used as a nonexhaustive coordinator, and *cetera* is a counterpart of the *pro* in (64c); like *a* in (65b), it does not occur in a minimal coordinate construction. For those who accept it, *et* is a normal conjunction, similar to *ji* 'and' in (67c).

(67)   a. I bought jam, bread, etc.   b. (*)I bought bread, etc.
       c. Wo   mai-le   mianbao ji   qita.   [Mandarin]
          I   buy-PRF bread   and   other
          'I bought bread and other things.'

A noniterative coordinator must occur in a minimal coordinate construction, but a nonexhaustive coordinator must not. The contrast is determined by the lexical properties of the coordinator. In the rest of this Element, we do not discuss these two types of coordinators anymore.

3.3.2 Coordinators in Larger Coordinate Constructions

In this subsection, we discuss two generalizations on the distributions of coordinators in constructions that have more than two conjuncts. The acceptability contrast between (68a) and (68b) leads to the first generalization in (69) (e.g., Dik 1968: 41, 58; Kayne 1994: 57; see Haspelmath 2004: 5 and Zhang 2010: 71–72 for similar examples in some other languages; cf. Mitrović 2014: 41).[11]

(68)   a.   I saw Audrey, James, **and** Lisa.   b.   *I saw Audrey, **and** James, Lisa.

(69)   Generalization 1: if there is only one overt coordinator, it must be next to the last conjunct in languages such as English and Mandarin.

If one assumes that coordinators have no syntactic status (e.g., Goodall 1987: 32) or they are adjuncts to conjuncts (e.g., Moltmann 1992: 25, 28), the assumption does not predict this generalization. If one assumes that every conjunct occurs with a coordinator and some of them may be deleted at PF (Moltmann 1992: 49) or have a null form (Johannessen 1998: §4.6), the assumption also cannot explain the generalization.

There are two approaches to Generalization 1. One is that there are multiple &P shells, and at LF, a coordinator moves from the lowest head position to the highest head position (Kayne 1994: 57; Zoerner 1995: 24), and thus, only the lowest copy is PF-visible. This is shown in (70a). According to Kayne, the phonetically unrealized head in (68a) is licensed by the LF raising of *and*. Since there is no parallel LF lowering, (68b) cannot be generated.

(70)   a.   b.

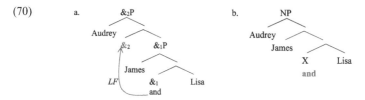

In (70a), *Lisa* is the complement of $\&_1$, and *James* is a Specifier of $\&_1$; $\&_1P$ is the complement of $\&_2$ and *Audrey* is a Specifier of $\&_2$. A complement is an element that a head is merged with for the first time, a Specifier is an element that a head is merged with after the complement, and more Specifiers can be merged after that (Chomsky 2002: 133; 2013: 42). Multiple Specifiers are seen in (70b), which is the other approach to (69). In this second approach (Zhang 2010), the unique head takes the last conjunct *Lisa* as its complement, and all nonfinal conjuncts are Specifiers of the unique coordinator.[12] In this approach, if the head took the middle conjunct *James* as its complement, *Lisa* would not be integrated. This explains the acceptability contrast between (68a) and (68b).

Also, if only one coordinator occurs in a multiple conjunct construction, it is impossible for some conjuncts to have a conjunctive relation and some others to have a disjunctive relation (Neeleman et al. 2023: 53). Since there is only one coordinator, both approaches explain this restriction.

We will see how the J-theory explains this generalization, after we introduce the second generalization.

The second generalization is (71) (Borsley 1994, 2005; Dougherty 1970: 858 (61)–(63), 860 (83); Winter 2001: 65 (99)):

(71)   Generalization 2: If there are three or more conjuncts, subgrouping is impossible unless each conjunct is next to an overt coordinator.

Borsley reports several observations to show this generalization. We introduce one of them here. In (72a), only one coordinator occurs, and in (72b), a coordinator occurs between every two conjuncts. Now consider their reading contrasts: (72b) has the four readings in (73), but (72a) has the first two readings only (Borsley 1994, 2005).

(72)   a. [Tom, Dick and Harry] lifted the piano.
         b. [Tom and Dick and Harry] lifted the piano.

(73)   a. 'Tom lifted the piano, Dick lifted the piano, and Harry lifted the piano.'
         b. 'Tom, Dick and Harry together lifted the piano.'
         c. 'Tom lifted the piano, and Dick and Harry together lifted the piano.'
         d. 'Tom and Dick together lifted the piano, and Harry lifted the piano.'

The contrast shows that a construction like (72a) is structurally different from (72b). If one assumes that every conjunct occurs with a coordinator and some of

---

[12] Zoerner (1995: 20; 1999: 324) and Zhang (2010) assumes that in a coordinate structure, category features are percolated from a Specifier to the whole complex. Thus, in (70b), the DP category is assumed to come from the Specifier *Audrey*. Although Spec-Head agreement is seen in other constructions, stipulating a categorial Specifier-Head dependency has not been independently observed.

them may be deleted or have a null form, the assumption cannot explain the generalization.

In the multiple coordinator construction (72b), there are two possible structures, as shown in (74a) and (74b). In (74a), the first *and* can also be pronounced as [*n*]; and in (74b), the second *and* can also be pronounced as [*n*] (Zoerner 1999: 328).

(74)   a. [[Tom and Dick] and Harry] lifted the piano.
         b. [Tom and [Dick and Harry]] lifted the piano.

Both the Spec-Complement theory (as in (70a)) and the J-theory can capture the availability of the four readings. In the Spec-Complement theory, if (72b) has the structure in (74a), the Specifier of the second *and* is an &P headed by the first *and*, as in (75a); if (72b) has the structure in (74b), the complement of the first *and* is an &P headed by the second *and*, as in (75b). In both (74a) and (74b), if both levels of coordinate relation are distributive, (73a) is reached; if both levels of coordinate relation are collective, (73b) is reached. Also, in (74a), if the matrix level of &P is distributive and the embedded &P is collective, (73d) is derived. On the other hand, in (74b), if the matrix level of &P is distributive and the embedded &P is collective, (73c) is derived.

(75)

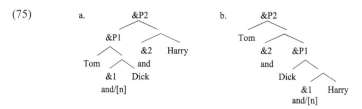

In the J-theory, in (74a), the J-set [*and Harry*] is integrated by the DP [*Tom and Dick*], in which the J-set [*and Dick*] is integrated by *Tom*, as in (76a). In (74b), *Tom* integrates the J-set *and* [*Dick and Harry*], where *Dick* integrates the J-set [*and Harry*], as in (76b).

(76)

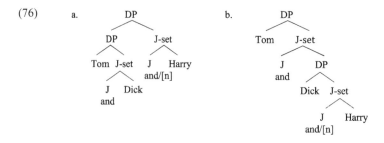

In both (76a) and (76b), if the coordinate relation is distributive in both levels, (73a) is reached; if the coordinate relation is collective in both levels, (73b) is reached. Also, the collective reading of the embedded coordination and the distributive reading of the matrix one in (76a) achieve (73d); and the collective reading of the embedded coordination and the distributive reading of the matrix one in (76b) achieve (73c). Therefore, (72b) allows four readings.

Thus, (72b) does not represent an independent pattern (contra the multiple branching symmetrical structure analysis in Neeleman et al. 2023), since it is structurally ambiguous: it can be either (74a) or (74b); and in both cases, there is one overt coordinator in each level.[13]

In the single coordinator construction (72a), the three conjuncts have either the distributive reading in (73a) or the collective reading in (73b). It is the lack of subgrouping of (72a) that distinguishes the analyses of (70a) and (70b). Although both the multiple &P shell analysis and the multiple Specifier analysis have a right-branching structure for such an example, as argued by Borsley (1994, 2005), if the last two conjuncts formed a maximal projection, &P, as seen in (70a), the subgrouping of the last two conjuncts (i.e., (73c)) would be possible, contrary to the fact. Zhang (2010: 74) thus claims that in (72a), the two nonfinal conjuncts are two Specifiers of the unique head that is realized by the coordinator, and thus (72a) has a structure similar to (70b). In this multiple-Specifier structure, the second and the last conjunct form an intermediate projection, which is not syntactically independent. Thus, these two conjuncts do not form a group semantically. Therefore, the multiple Specifier analysis can, but the &P-shell analysis cannot, explain the unavailability of the reading (73c) for (72a). Thus, the former approach is superior to the latter in explaining Generalization 2.

Of course, in neither analysis do the first two conjuncts form a constituent. Thus, both explain the unavailability of the reading (73d) for (72a). Moreover, in both analyses, the possible distributive relation of the three conjuncts gives (73a), and possible collective relation of the three conjuncts gives (73b), for (72a). There is no flat multitermed structure, contra Neeleman et al. (2023: 64 f).

---

[13] Kayne (1994: 145, n. 11; see his references) addresses repetitive coordination constructions like those in (i), where the first *and* must occur. As stated in Gleitman (1965: 293), "such repetitions have the effect of suggesting continuous or repeated or increasing action." Verb reduplication to denote iterative actions or events without a coordinator is seen in many languages, for example, Madurese (Davies 2000). (ii) is an example in Mandarin (Zhang 2015). We do not discuss such constructions.

(i)   a.   John read and read and read.   b.   I hit him and hit him and hit him — until he died.
(ii)   A-Gui   zai   jia-li   qiao-qiao-da-da.
        A-Gui   at   home-in   RED.knock-beat
        'A-Gui beat something repeatedly at home.'

In the J-theory, the lack of subgrouping in the single coordinator construction is explained as follows. The unique J, which is realized by *and*, takes the last conjunct *Harry* as its complement, and the built cluster takes *Dick* as its Specifier, forming a complex J-set, as shown in (77). Specifier is defined as the second element for a head to merge with (Chomsky 2002: 133; 2013: 42). In (77), the complex J-set is merged with and integrated by *Tom*. In this structure, since *Dick* is inside a J-set, it does not categorize the containing J-set. It is *Tom* that categorizes the complex J-set.

(77)   [NP [NP Tom] [J-set [NP Dick] [and Harry]]]

As stated, in (77), although *Dick* and [*and Harry*] form a constituent, this constituent is a J-set, which has no syntactic category and thus is not syntactically independent. Accordingly, these two conjuncts do not form a group semantically. Also, in (77), the possible distributive relation of the three conjuncts gives (73a), and possible collective relation of the three conjuncts gives (73b), for (72a). This explains Generalization 2 in the same way as the multiple Specifier analysis.

Moreover, in (77), there is only one J element, which is *and*. This J element takes the last conjunct, rather than any other conjunct, as its complement. This explains Generalization 1 in the same way as the multiple Specifier analysis.

A similar complex J-set is also seen in the formation of compounds (Zhang 2022).

The same analysis applies to larger coordinate constructions, such as (78a) (=(66b)), whose structure is (78b). The J in the top J-set is null, which introduces a complex modifier to *someone*. The modifier has four AP conjuncts.

(78)   a. I met someone young, happy, eager to go to college, and tired of wasting time.

　　　　　b.

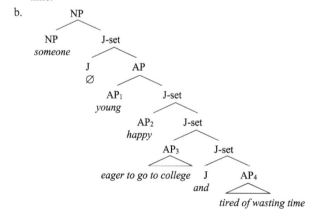

This recursive merger of a J-set in a multiple conjunct construction explains at least two facts. One is that no subgrouping is possible, as discussed. The other is that it is impossible for two of the conjuncts to have a conjunctive relation and the others to have a disjunctive relation. This is because the same J element never has two sets of different properties.

3.4 Shared Properties of Coordinators and Modification Markers

English does not have modification markers, but some other languages do (Rubin 1994, 2003). The Mandarin modification marker *de* occurs between elements of various categories that have a modification relation, as seen in (79) (Zhang 2010: 95–96; we do not discuss *de* in nonmodification constructions):[14]

(79)　　a. Yani　qiaoqiao-**de**　likai-le.　　　　　　*Manner Adv*
　　　　　　Yani　quietly-MOD　leave-PRF
　　　　　　'Yani left quietly.'

　　　　b. Na-ge　**pangpang-de**　nahai　you　lai-le.　*Adjective*
　　　　　　that-CL　fat-MOD　　　boy　again　come-PRF
　　　　　　'That fat boy came again.'

　　　　c. Na-ge　likai-**de**　nanhai　you　lai-le.　*Relative clause*
　　　　　　that-CL　leave-MOD　boy　again　come-PRF
　　　　　　'The boy who had left came again.'

　　　　d. Yani　kanjian-le　ji-jia　　yan　malu-**de**　shangdian.　*PP*
　　　　　　Yani　see-PRF　several-CL　along　road-MOD　shop
　　　　　　'Yani saw several shops along the road.'

　　　　e. Yani　mei　kanjian　qita-**de**　shangdian.　*Scope-taking Adj*
　　　　　　Yani　not　see　　other-MOD　shop
　　　　　　'Yani did not see the other shops.'

There are seven shared properties of coordinators and modification markers such as *de* in (79). First, like pure functional elements such as C and T, neither has a theta relation with another element.

Second, like other functional elements, both are a closed set.

Third, both must be associated with at least two elements: one links a modifier to a modified element, and the other links one conjunct to another conjunct.

Fourth, neither has any category features. *And* does not project any categorial features, nor does the modification marker *de* in Mandarin (Li 2008). In (79), *de* occurs in various categorial contexts. Based on this and the third shared

---

[14]　Larson (2018) claims that *de* with a modifier in Mandarin is a case concordializer. But Li (2022: 174) points out that many modifiers do not contain any nominal, for example, *pangpang-de* 'fat' in (79b), challenging Larson's claim.

property, Li (2008) finds that the syntactic behaviors of *de* and *and* are almost identical (also see Zhang 2010: 97).

Fifth, like many functional heads, both can be silent in a language or in certain constructions of a language. J is null in modification constructions in English. We have seen null coordinator constructions in (57). For nonexhaustive coordinators, a null version is available in both English and Mandarin (Section 3.3.1). In Mandarin, a null modification marker in seen in examples like (80).

(80)   <u>Congming   ren</u>   bu   gan   na-zhong shi.
         wise   person   not   do   that-kind thing
        'Wise people do not do that kind of thing.'

Sixth, both appear in a linker position. We have seen the linker position of the modification markers in (49) through (52). The Mandarin modification marker *de* may precede or follow a modifier of a verbal expression, as seen in (81a) and (81b), respectively, and in (82a) and (82b), respectively (also see Li 2022).

(81)   a. Alan ^{H}shuo-^{M}de   hen man.[15]
            Alan   speak-MOD   very slow
         b. Alan hen man-^{M}de ^{H}shuo.
            Both a and b: 'Alan spoke slowly.'

(82)   a. Alan   huida-de   hen   zhengque.
            Alan   answer-MOD   very   correct
            'Alan answered question correctly.'
         b. Alan   hen zhengque-de   huida-le   yi-ge   wenti.
            Alan   very correct-MOD   answer-PRF   one-CL   question
            'Alan answered a question correctly.'

Whereas the form variation of a linker is exhibited in the phonological forms in (52), it is exhibited in the written forms of *de* in Mandarin. The linker that precedes a nominal Head, as in (79b–e), is 的; the one that precedes a verbal Head, as in (79a), (81b), and (82b), is 地, and the one that follows the Head, as in (81a) and (82a), is 得. The different written forms in Mandarin correlate with different phonological forms in some dialects (e.g., in Cantonese, the three forms are *ge, gam,* and *dak,* respectively; Zhu 1980: 162).

Morphologically, all these *de*s in Mandarin are enclitic (cf. Huang 1989), similar to the Japanese conjunction *-to*. Like *-to* in (55b), *de* cannot occur at the left-edge of a prosodic word. Parallel to the coordinators in (46a) and (46b), if a modification marker introduces a modifier to the modified element, it forms a

---

[15] Multiple modifiers may occur preverbally, but at most one modifier may occur postverbally. This is captured by Huang's (1984: 54) constraint that "a verb in Chinese may be followed by at most one constituent, though it may be preceded by an indefinite number of constituents (including subject and adverbial modifiers)."

constituent with the modifier; and thus, in both (81a) and (81b), *de* forms a syntactic constituent with *hen man* 'very slow.' The syntactic constituency boundary matches the prosodic boundary in (81b), as shown in (83a), but not in (81a), as shown in (83b).

(83)   a.   b.

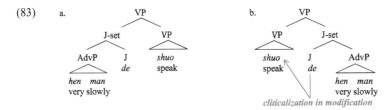

cliticalization in modification

Seventh, if there are more than two elements and only one coordinator or modification marker occurs, it must be next to the final element. We saw the constraint on coordinators in (68). (84) shows the same constraint on the modification marker *de* in Mandarin.

(84)   a. Alan mai-le yi-ge hen xiao, hen qing, hen bo-**de**   shouji.
          Alan buy-PRF one-CL very small very light very thin-MOD cellphone
          'Alan bought a very small, very light, and very thin cellphone.'
       b. *Alan mai-le yi-ge hen xiao, hen qing-**de**, hen bo shouji.

In addition to the seven shared properties of coordinators and modification markers, not surprisingly, the two kinds of formatives may share the same form in some languages. The Classical Chinese word *er* is used as a conjunction in (85a), but a modification marker in (85b). The same linker also has multiple uses in several Formosan languages (Tsai & Wu 2012). The linker *ru'* is a conjunction in (86a) and a modification marker to introduce a purpose expression in (86b) (Tsai & Wu 2012: 167).

(85)   a. xia   liang **er**   dong   wen   [Classical Chinese]
          summer cool   and   winter warm
          'Summer is cool and winter is warm.'
       b. Zilu   shuai'er **er**   dui
          Zilu   carelessly MOD   answer
          'Zilu answered carelessly.'

(86)   a. S<um>'an eu' bauwak 'i' Tapas [**ru'** hab-un=nia'].   [Mayarinax]
          breed<AV> ACC wild.hog NOM Tapas LK   kill-PV=3.SL.OBL
          'Tapas bred hogs and then killed them.'
       b. S<um>'an [**ru'** pahab] cu'   bauwak   'i'   Tapas.
          breed<AV> LK   kill   ACC wild.hog NOM   Tapas
          'Tapas bred hogs to kill.'

In this section, I have presented systematic shared properties of coordinators and modification markers. It is unlikely that the two kinds of formatives share all these seven properties by accident. On the other hand, no other kinds of syntactic elements have all of these properties together. As I claimed in Section 2, they both are J elements.

3.5 Summary

In this section, I have argued for the following with respect to the syntax of coordinators. A. Coordinators may have c-selection. B. Their morphological position is that of a linker. C. An additional coordinator in a binary coordination is a focus marker, instead of a J element. D. There are two less-studied types of coordinators: noniterative and nonexhaustive ones. E. In a construction with more than two conjuncts, if only one coordinator occurs, the lowest conjunct is the complement of J, the highest one is a categorizer of the J-set, and the rest conjuncts are Specifiers of J; however, if every conjunct is next to a coordinator, the construction is structurally ambiguous. F. Both coordinators and modification markers are realizations of J. This conclusion again reaches a unified analysis of coordinate and modification constructions (see Section 2.3).

4 Removing Construction-Specific Syntactic Operations

We have seen how a coordinate complex is built in syntax. Our next question is whether there is any special constraint in the building. Can any syntactic type of element be free in internal and external merge in other constructions but not in a coordinate construction? Many scholars have recognized a negative answer to the question, to be introduced in this section.

4.1 Understanding the External Merge in Coordination

4.1.1 A Wide Range of the Categories and Category Levels of Conjuncts

In this section, I address the issue of whether a conjunct must be a particular syntactic category and category level.

According to the clausal conjunct hypothesis (CCH), conjuncts must be clauses (Gleitman 1965; Chomsky 1957: §5.2; Ross 1967; Tai 1969; cf. Wilder 1997: 63; Johannessen 1998). Zhang (2010: 65ff.) summarizes some problems of the CCH. Altshuler and Truswell (2022: 15–19) also present arguments against the CCH. However, Schein (2017) reexamines some of the arguments in the literature, including the issues of collective predicates, number agreement, quantified nominal conjuncts, and asymmetrical coordination, claiming that none of them falsifies the CCH.

Schein's (2017) new version of the CCH is event semantics-oriented. In his analysis, (87a), for example, has the semantics in (87b), which tells us that there is an event *e*, the sauce *s* participates in this event and the cheese *c* also participates in this event, and this event is a perfect marriage. The nominal coordination *the sauce and the cheese* in (87a) thus has unspoken relations. From (87b), we can see that "the ordinary sentential connective conjoins clauses about the sauce's and the cheese's participation in the same event" (p. 1).

(87)   a. At Acropolis Pizza, the sauce and the cheese are a perfect marriage of two rivals.

         b. For some event e, ((Participates(e, s) and Participates(e, c)) & be a perfect marriage(e))

            'The sauce participates and the cheese participates & it's a perfect marriage.'

Basically, the new version of the CCH assumes that each individual denoted by a nominal conjunct participates in an event, and thus this conjunct should be understood as a sentence, instead of a nominal. Schein (2017: 2) further states that "If *and* is always a sentential connective, then much of what it connects often goes unspoken — Conjunction Reduction (Chomsky 1957; Ross 1967) — and unspoken must be grasped in context from what is not unspoken."

In my approach, I do not assume that syntactic structures have to cover such a participation relation. One issue that is not addressed in the CCH so far is the possible c-selection of coordinators (Section 3.2). Welmers (1973: 305) states that he is not aware of any African language that expresses nominal and clausal coordination in the same way. If all conjuncts are, or are derived from, clausal conjuncts, it is hard to explain the syntactic distributions of these coordinators. Also, it is not clear how the CCH explains the possible syntactic differences of the left conjunct in a nominal and a clausal coordination (Section 2.2). Furthermore, in a Hydra, such as (88) (Section 5.4), if the coordinate nominal came from two clauses, the relative pronoun of the restrictive relative clause would fail to have an antecedent, since such a relative clause modifies a nominal only.

(88)   a man and a woman who knew each other well

Also, in (89) (Section 5.5), it is unlikely for the conjuncts in the constituent *k* to be two clauses, in addition to the clausal conjuncts linked by the second *and*.

(89)   [The dogs and the roosters]$_k$ barked and crowed all night.

As for the category levels of conjuncts, we address two points. First, a conjunct can be a nonphrasal element, such as a single word or a part of a word. Thus, two transitive verbs can be conjoined, sharing a direct object.

Kayne (1994) claims that conjuncts must be phrases and apparent word-level coordination involves conjoined phrases to which a deletion process has applied. Consider, however, (90a) and (91), which have been discussed in Jackendoff (1977: 192) and Borsley (2005: 471).

(90)   a. Hobbs whistled and hummed a total of sixteen tunes.
         b. Hobbs whistled a total of 16 tunes and hummed a total of sixteen tunes.

(91)   a. Hobbs whistled and hummed the same tune.
         b. Hobbs criticized and insulted many people.

In (90a), for instance, there are sixteen tunes involved, whereas in (90b), there are thirty-two tunes involved. Obviously, it is impossible for (90a) to be derived from (90b) by deletion, since deletion must obey the recoverability condition on interpretation (Chomsky 1965). The examples in (91) show the same point. Based on such data, Borsley (2005: Section 4) finds Kayne's deletion analysis of word coordination problematic. Instead, verbs can be conjuncts. Takano (2004) uses similar arguments to show that verb conjuncts also exist in Japanese. Also see Schein (2017: 107, 835 n. 16) for a discussion.

Petzell (2017), however, finds that Borsley's argument against Kayne's from the deletion perspective is not effective. According to him, if the apparent verb coordination is derived by the following three steps, the conjuncts can still be phrasal. Step 1, two VPs that have the same object are conjoined. Step 2, the objects in both conjuncts undergo ATB movement (non-reconstructable). Step 3, the remnant coordinate VP moves. I use (92) to illustrate the structure of (91b) in this analysis. In (92), the underlined conjuncts are two VPs, rather than two verbs.

(92)   Hobbs [criticized t_i and insulted t_j]$_k$ [many people]$_j$ t_k.

Petzell then finds another way to show the existence of verb conjuncts. He shows that, in Old Swedish, if a word undergoes a stylistic fronting, it lands at a position right next to a complementizer. But a phrase cannot do so. Importantly, a verb conjunct can show up in that position. He thus concludes that conjuncts can be a word.

In addition to Petzell's argument, other kinds of argument can also support the existence of word conjuncts. In the three steps of the derivation in (92), if we can find a construction in which the second step is impossible but two verbal conjuncts still share an object, the construction must be a verb, rather than a VP, coordinate construction. In Mandarin, an indefinite WH-object cannot undergo any movement, as shown in (93b). Since the movement of *shenme-dongxi* 'something' in (93c) is impossible, the coordinate complex *mǎi-le you mài-le* 'bought and sold' there cannot be a phrase that has undergone a remnant movement. The acceptability of such an example also indicates the existence of verb conjuncts.

(93)   a. Lulu haoxiang măi-le   shenmen-dongxi.
            Lulu seem   buy-PRF   what-thing
            'Lulu seems to have bought something.'
        b. *Shenme-dongxi   Lulu haoxiang măi-le.
        c. Lulu haoxiang [măi-le   you mài-le]   shenme-dongxi.
            Lulu seem   buy-PRF   and sell-PRF   what-thing
            'Lulu seems to have bought something and then sold it.'

Bresnan and Thráinsson (1990) also argue for the existence of verb coordination in Icelandic, which is independent of verb phrase coordination and ellipsis constructions. Te Velde (2005) also argues for the existence of verb conjuncts in some Germanic languages. Also see Zoerner (1999: 339) and de Vries (2005: 91 n. 7). In addition to verb conjuncts, (94) has noun conjuncts (see Heycock & Zamparelli 2003 for more examples).

(94)   [Dogs and cats] are equally filthy.

In examples like (94), the coordinate complex cannot come from any ellipsis. If we exclude the coordinate complexes that may come from ellipsis, we still can find a wide range of the category level for conjuncts. The existence of nonphrasal conjuncts and coordinate compounds may help us to get a deeper understanding of the relation between a syntactic structure and sizes of the elements therein (see Zhang 2010: 37). In Zoerner's Spec-Complement relation between conjuncts, "& stands as a completely feature-neutral syntactic head. Since it has no a priori syntactic features, it does not have to have complements or specifiers of any particular type" (Zoerner 1999: 339). This is compatible with the J-theory: J does not have to have complements or its categorizers of any particular type.

The second issue that needs to be clarified is that there is no conjunct of intermediate projection, that is, the sister of a Specifier is not a coordinate complex (Bošković 2020b: 152). For example, (95a) is not derived from (95b), which has T′-conjuncts (Salzman 2015: 12 (48), *sic*).

(95)   a. John has bought a new car but will certainly sell it soon.
        b. John [$_T$′ has ~~John~~ bought a new car] but [$_T$′ will certainly <John> sell it soon].

It is widely assumed that an intermediate projection is not syntactically independent: it cannot move, for example. In (95a), the second conjunct [*will certainly sell it soon*] starts with the modal *will*. The reading of the subject of the clause is *John*, which is not next to the modal. If a conjunct is never an intermediate projection, the category level of this conjunct cannot be T′. According to Bošković (2020b), both conjuncts here are full TPs (or IPs), and the subject is in the Specifier of a higher projection.

Having discussed the computation of basic coordinate constructions in the previous sections, in this section I have addressed the constraints on the computation. Regarding the category levels of conjuncts (a size issue), I do not exclude the ellipsis possibility in conjuncts. There is quite a lot of literature on the ellipsis in coordinate constructions. But still, the syntax of the construction before any ellipsis is more fundamental. What I have shown in this section is the reality of the various levels of conjuncts without any ellipsis. I conclude that neither the complement of J, nor the element that is merged with a J-set, is restricted to any category or category level, although neither can be an intermediate projection.

4.1.2 Categorial Relations between Conjuncts and the RPR

There are various constraints specifically designed for the relations between conjuncts. Chomsky (1957: 36, 1965: 212 n. 9) claims that different categories cannot be conjoined (but see (7a)). This is the coordination of likes constraint (CLC) (also Bloomfield 1933: 195; Williams 1981: §2; Gazdar 1981: 172). Schachter's (1977) coordinate constituent constraint (CCC) further states that conjuncts must not only belong to the same syntactic category but also have the same semantic function. Sag et al. (1985: 143), Goodall (1987: 43), and Munn (1993) claim that conjuncts must be identical only in semantic types. Peterson (2004: 650) claims that conjuncts should be identical in grammatical functions (such as OBJECT, ADJUNCT, and PREDICATE). Various versions of the CLC have been also proposed in other works. See Zhang (2010: Ch. 7) for a review.

In reality, more cases of coordinate constructions with syntactically unlike conjuncts are reported, cross-linguistically (e.g., Patejuk & Przepiórkowski 2023; Przepiórkowski 2022a), and even in sign languages (Zorzi 2018: 133). This is also true of derived coordinate complexes, such as the clause-initial *kto i začem* 'who and why' in (96) (Kazenin 2002) (see Section 5.2)

(96)　　[Kto i　　začem]　prixodil?　[Russian]
　　　　who and　why　　came
　　　　'Who came and for what reason?'

Nobody has claimed that unlike conjuncts are always possible. See Borsley (2005: 464) for impossible examples. After reviewing various constraints on conjuncts proposed in the literature, Zhang (2010) proposes a general filter on the representations of syntactic complexes:

(97)   Parts of a complex must hold a coherence relation in terms of:
   a. Relatedness: they must be related to each other semantically; or
   b. Resemblance: they must hold a resemblance relation in terms of their semantic type and their dependency chains.

The notion of coherence is adapted from Kehler (2002). I group various kinds of coherence relations into my general Relatedness relation. If the resemblance requirement is a parallelism requirement (PR), the coherence filter in (97) is a relativized parallelism requirement (RPR).

In a modification construction, the modification relation between the components satisfies the Relatedness part of the RPR by definition. A coordinate construction differs from a modification one in the sense that the two parts do not have to be semantically related. The RPR captures an inclusively disjunctive coherence relation between conjuncts. In other words, conjuncts must satisfy either the Relatedness stated in (97a) or the resemblance stated in (97b), or both. Also, the two kinds of coherence relation are independent of each other, and they are equally important. For example, in (98a), although the two conjuncts are not related, they are both embedded questions, that is, they are of the same semantic type; in (98b), although the first conjunct is nominal and second one is a clause, they are semantically related: the first conjunct encodes a condition for the second conjunct.

(98)   a. I wonder who$_i$ [John saw t$_i$] and [Peter thinks t$_i$ kissed Mary].   (Bošković 2022a: 4)
   b. One more can of beer and I'm leaving.   (Culicover & Jackendoff 1997: 196)

Unlike the representation filter in (97), any special constraint on the operations applied to conjuncts is ad hoc. Given the general operation of Merge, unlike categories can conjoin. In the J-theory, the complement of J does not have to be categorially and structurally the same as the integrator of the J-set. Both parts of the RPR, Relatedness and Resemblance, reflect the economy in processing, rather than a constraint on the operations in building a coordinate complex. See Zhang (2010: Ch. 7) for more discussion of the nonsyntactic nature of the RPR.[16]

---

[16] The issue of number agreement in coordination and modification constructions in English is discussed in Zhang (2010: 130–132), among many others. One basic fact is that in both constructions, both singular and plural agreement can be triggered, and the choice does not seem to be totally decided by the syntactic structure. See Kučerová and Munn (2023) for the claim that agreement is both syntactic and postsyntactic.

4.2 Understanding the Internal Merge in Coordination

Ross's (1967: 89) coordinate structure constraint (CSC) states: "In a coordination structure, no conjunct may be moved, nor may any element contained in a conjunct be moved out of that conjunct." The first and second part of the CSC are called conjunct constraint (CC) and element constraint (EC), respectively (Grosu 1973). The CSC was intended as a linguistic universal and is a construction-specific constraint on movement. I discuss the two parts of the CSC in the following two subsections, respectively.

4.2.1 Conjunct Constraint

The CC states that no conjunct may move. See Zhang (2010: §4.1.2) for a review of various analyses of this part of the CSC. However, if a conjunct is not a root, it is categorized, and thus it should be able to move. Indeed, conjuncts can move in Serbo-Croatian (Bošković 2022a: 13), as seen in (99):

(99)   ?Knjige$_i$ je   Marko [t$_i$ i   filmove]   kupio   [Serbo-Croatian]
        books   is   Marko   and   movies   bought
        'Marko bought books and movies.'

Conjunct movement is also found in Classical Greek, Latin, and Russian (Agbayani et al. 2011: 234), Polish (Prażmowska 2013: (25c), (26c)) and the many languages mentioned in Oda (2017, 2021) and Bošković (2020a) (also see Altshuler & Truswell 2022: 42–44). See Bošković's and Oda's works for various possible constraints on such movement. Like the movement of other kinds of elements, the movement of conjuncts may have spell-out traces (i.e., one type of resumptive pronouns) in some languages. For example, in the Igbo (100b), the second conjunct undergoes focus fronting, leaving the resumptive pronoun *yá* in the base-position (Georgi & Amaechi 2020: (8), (21); *rV* is a suffix, where *V* means vowel). Georgi and Amaechi exclude the base-generation possibility of the left focused element in such an example.

(100)   a. Ézè hù-rù [Òbí nà Àdá].   b. Àdá kà Ézè hù-rù [Òbí nà yá].
            Eze see-rv Obi and Ada   Ada FOC Eze see-rv Obi and 3SG
            'Ézè saw Òbí and Àdá.'   'Ézè saw Òbí and ÀDÁ.'

Also, according to Petzell (2017), the first conjunct of a [V & VP] construction can move in some Germanic languages.

Moreover, since coordinators and modification markers are clitics, as expected, a modifier and a modified element cannot both move, stranding the modification marker, and the conjuncts of a coordination construction also cannot both move, stranding the coordinator.

But what we must address is the following: if a J-set has no category, why can it move in some languages? In English, the combination of a coordinator and the conjunct to its right cannot move, as seen in (101) (Sledd 1959: 101) (see more examples in Zhang 2010: 22):

(101) a. The rain stopped <u>and they finished the second game</u>.
      b. *<u>And they finished the second game</u> the rain stopped.

However, in the Japanese example in (102a) (Oda 2021: 606), the combination of the first conjunct and the enclitic coordinator *-to* 'and' moves. Similarly, in the Mandarin example in (102b), the combination of the modifier and the enclitic modification marker *de* moves. In both cases, a J-set is away from its base-position.

(102) a. ?Kyoodai$_i$-to   kanojo-wa [t$_i$ Toodai]-ni   akogareteiru.
         Kyoto.University-and she-TOP   Tokyo.University-DAT admire
         'She admires Kyoto University and also Tokyo University.'
      b. Jijimangmang-de$_i$ Alan   t$_i$ qu-le   yiyuan.
         hurry-MOD   Alan   go-PRF   hospital
         'Alan went to the hospital in a hurry.'

According to Oda (2017) and Bošković (2020a), in (102a), "the conjunction cliticizes to the first conjunct and is in fact carried along under the movement of the first conjunct" (Bošković 2020a: 248). In (102b), *de* is also an enclitic; and when the modifier moves, *de* goes with its morphological host. The J element in such a case is like the negative bound form *n't* in English: *n't* moves with an auxiliary, although the free form *not* cannot do so, as seen in (103). In (103a), the moving cluster *hasn't* is not a constituent. We thus assume that the apparent movement of a J-set in examples like those in (102) might have a similar morphosyntactic account as the movement of *hasn't* in (103a), whatever it is.

(103) a.   Hasn't the potion worked?   b.   Has the potion not worked?
       c.   *Has not the potion worked?

4.2.2 Element Constraint

Asymmetrical coordination examples like (104) and (105) (Culicover & Jackendoff 1997) typically do not show the EC effect of the CSC, which bans the movement of any element from a conjunct (Ross 1967). Bošković (2020b) reviews that the EC is observed in some languages, but not others.

(104) Here's the whisky which I [[went to the store] and [bought]].   (Ross 1967: 168)

(105)   a. What kind of cancer can you eat herbs and not get?
         b. What kind of herbs can you eat and not get cancer?

In Zhang (2010), the EC effects in languages such as English are explained by
the RPR (see (97)) (also see Kehler 2002: 103–117, Oda 2021). According to
Altshuler and Truswell (2022), EC, as well as adjunct islands, may have some
nonsyntactic accounts. McInnerney and Sugimono (2022) also argue that island
effects have both syntactic and nonsyntactic sources.

On the other hand, there are general properties reflected in both the EC and
the adjunct island effects. For example, Bošković's research (2020a: 238f.)
shows that the EC can be violated if the head of the construction moves (cf.
Georgi & Amaechi 2020), and the same effect can be observed in adverbial and
other constructions.

4.3 Summary

In this section, integrating some updated research, I have strengthened the
theory that there is no universal coordinate construction-specific syntactic
operations. As in other constructions, elements of various categories and
category-levels can undergo external and internal merge in principle. The
operations all obey the general rules and are subject to some nonsyntactic
(e.g., the RPR) and language-specific restrictions.

5 Movement Modes in Deriving Certain Coordinate Constructions

In the previous sections, I have argued that there is no syntactic operation or
constraint exclusively applied to coordination. This means that the building of
various coordinate constructions is not special. This is true not only in the
constructions discussed in the previous sections, but also in other constructions.
In this section, I explore the derivations of five coordinate constructions, as
shown in (106). Some of them have not been well-studied in the literature.

(106)   a. I wonder who John saw _ and Bill hit _.
         b. [Kada   i   gde]   si   ih   video?   [Serbo-Croatian]
            when   and   where   2SG.AUX   them   saw
            'When and where did you see them?'
         c. [The dogs and the roosters] barked and crowed all night.
         d. Mary met a man$_i$ and John met a woman$_j$ [who$_{i\&j}$ knew each other $_{i\&j}$ well].
         e. Italy borders France.

In (106a), both conjuncts contain a gap, and the left-edge *who* is semantically
associated with the gaps. In (106b), in the clause-initial coordinate complex, the
two conjuncts are associated with the time and location of the event denoted by

the clause, respectively. In (106c), we see two coordinate complexes: a nominal one on the left (*the dogs and the roosters*) and a verbal one on the right (*barked and crowed*). *The dogs* seems to function as the subject of *barked*, and *the roosters* seems to function as the subject of *crowed*. In (106d), each underlined part is contained in a clausal conjunct, but the two parts together are modified by the relative clause at the right end. In these four constructions, we see various semantic links in coordinate complexes. How are the links represented in syntax? In (106e), there is no coordinator, but the subject and the object are thematically parallel. Is this construction derived from a hidden coordinate complex, *Italy and France*? I show that the derivations of the five constructions do not need any coordination-specific operations or constraints.

5.1 Across-the-Board Construction

5.1.1 Three Types

An across-the-board (ATB) construction is a construction in which each clausal conjunct contains a gap, and a left-edge element is associated with the gaps semantically. Two examples are in (107).

(107)   a. I wonder <u>who</u> John saw _ and Bill hit _.
        b. This is <u>the brush</u> that John used _ for cleaning the toilet and Mary used _ for cleaning the kitchen.

In (107a), for example, the gaps in the two conjuncts are identical in interpretation, and they both are linked to *who*. The speaker asks for the information about the same person that John saw and Bill hit. I call this kind of ATB construction identical across-the-board (I-ATB) construction.

In (108a), however, the gaps in the two conjuncts are not identical in interpretation. Imagine that Bill and Fred each have their own list of targets. (108a) can be answered by (108b) or (108c) (Munn 1999: 422).

(108)   a. Which man did Bill kill _ on Tuesday and Fred kill _ on Wednesday?
        b. Bill killed his first victim and Fred killed his second.
        c. Bill killed Bruno and Fred killed Arno.

A construction similar to (108a) is (109) in its sloppy reading, that is, Holland hates his own picture and Putin loves his own picture (de Vries 2017: 28):

(109)   Pictures of himself, Holland hates _ and Putin loves _.

An ATB construction like (108a) and (109) is understood as a respectively, nonidentity, or paired reading ATB construction. I call this kind of ATB construction respective across-the-board (R-ATB) construction. As noted by de Vries (2017: 27), the occurrence of an R-ATB construction depends on a plausible discourse, rather than on any specific morphosyntactic context (*pace* Zhang 2010; cf. Moltmann 1992: §2.4.2).

Finally, in (110), the gaps in the two conjuncts do not have the same interpretation as the left-edge phrase, although they are still associated with the phrase in a collective way (Abbott 1976; Gawron & Kehler 2004; Chaves 2012).

(110)   a. <u>A total of ten books</u> have been bought by Ken and stolen by Kim.
         b. It was <u>a total of $3000</u> that I borrowed and my sister stole from the bank.

Note that this construction has two clausal conjuncts, instead of two verb or predicate conjuncts as in *Hobbs sang and hummed a total of sixteen tunes* (see Section 4.1.1). The speaker of (110a) and (110b) does not care about the exact reading of each object gap in the coordinate complex, and thus we do not know whether the two gaps have the same interpretation. What we know is simply that the left-edge phrase must scope over the whole coordinate complex. I call this kind of ATB construction synthetic across-the-board (S-ATB) construction.

Multiple gap representations are not restricted to coordinate constructions, as observed in parasitic gap (PG) constructions, for example, (111b) (Munn 1992: 3).

(111)   a. Which paper did John file _ and Mary read _?
         b. Which paper did John file _ before Mary read _?

The relations between ATB and PG constructions have been studied by many, as reviewed by de Vries (2017). Some studies (e.g. Ting, to appear) report certain cross-linguistic facts to support a unified analysis of the two constructions. Restricted by space, I do not discuss PGs in this Element.

Two major issues must be addressed in the syntax of ATB constructions: the syntactic relation between the two gaps in the conjuncts, and the syntactic relation between the gaps and the left-edge overt phrase. The three kinds of ATB constructions exhibit different properties in these two aspects, and thus any unified approach is challenged. In the next section, I develop three available analyses and apply each of them only to one of the three kinds of ATB constructions (I-ATB, R-ATB, and S-ATB).

5.1.2 Non-unified Analysis of Various Across-the-Board Dependencies

In an I-ATB construction, the two gaps and the left-edge overt element are identical in interpretation. In internal merge, the two copies created must be "absolutely identical in every respect" (Chomsky 2019: 43). One plausible analysis of the construction is that the gap in the higher conjunct is a copy of the left-edge element, created by internal merge, and the gap in the other conjunct is a null proform (cf. Frank 1992; Munn 1992, 1993; Zhang 2010). A simplified structure of (112a) (= (107a)) is (112b), where the left-edge *who* and the one in the angle brackets are copies of an internal merge. As usual, the low copy is not overt. The gap in the second conjunct is a null proform, licensed by and interpreted the same as, <*who*> in the other conjunct.

(112) a. I wonder who [John saw _ and Bill hit _].
       b. I wonder who [[John saw <who>] [$_{J\text{-set}}$ and [Bill hit *pro*]]]

The two gaps of an I-ATB construction do not have to be of the same syntactic position. In (113), the first gap is for an object and the second one is for a subject.

(113) I know the man who [John likes_] and [we hope __ will win]   (Williams 1978: 34)

The gaps in an I-ATB also do not need to be nominal, either, as seen in (114). The proform in the second conjunct is a *pro*-vP in (114a), a *pro*-DegP in (114b), and a *pro*-AdvP in (114c).

(114) a. Burn a book Mary would never but John often does.   (cf. Salzman 2015: 4)
       b. How fast did John speak and Mary write during the meeting?   (de Vries 2017: 23)
       c. Never has Peter eaten pork or Mike drunk alcohol.   (de Vries 2017: 23)

The I-ATB construction can have other varieties. (115) is from Lakoff (1986), where the middle conjunct does not have a gap parallel to the other two conjuncts. Note that as in the examples of EC violation (see Section 4.2.2), the conjuncts in (115) are semantically related.

(115) How many courses can you take _ for credit, still stay sane, and get all A's in _?

The existence of such a nonexhaustive ATB construction challenges any analysis that assumes that conjuncts must be symmetrical (cf. Section 2.1).

All of these varieties of the I-ATB constructions can be explained in the proform analysis.

In contrast to an I-ATB construction, the gaps in the two conjuncts in an R-ATB construction, such as (116) (= (108a)), do not have the same interpretation.

(116) Which man did Bill kill $_1$ on Tuesday and Fred kill $_2$ on Wednesday?

In Chomsky (2019, 2021), elements in the same form but with different readings can be repetitions made by external merge, instead of copies made by internal merge. I thus claim that in such a construction, the elements in the two gap positions are repetitions, and ellipsis occurs in each conjunct. As we saw in (108), the question in (108a) has two answers in either (108b) or (108c). I claim that an R-ATB question, unlike any I-ATB question, asks two questions. The construction can be analyzed in an ellipsis approach (cf. e.g., Sjoblem 1980: 28ff.; George 1980; Wilder 1994; Salzman 2012, 2015). A simplified structure of (116) is (117), where *which man₁* and *which man₂* are repetitions, both are raised locally, their lower copy is not overt, and the strikethrough part is deleted because its form can be restored from the preceding conjunct.[17]

(117)   [Which man₁ did Bill kill <which man₁> on Tuesday] [J-set and [which man₂ did Fred kill <which man₂> on Wednesday]]

In the S-ATB construction, such as (118) (= (110a)), the left-edge expression semantically scopes over the combination of the two conjuncts, rather than either of the two conjuncts alone.

(118)   A total of ten books have been bought by Ken and stolen by Kim.

S-ATB constructions can also include examples like (119a), which has a different interpretation from the non-ATB construction in (119b). (119a) means that there are few politicians who both behave morally and are praised by their family members. It makes no statement about the number of moral politicians and the number of the politicians who are praised by their family members. This statement is made in (119b): both are not many. Thus, if the shared *few politicians* in the ATB construction in (119a) is reconstructed into both conjuncts, as in (119b), the meaning is changed. See McNally (1992: 337) and Fox and Johnson (2016) for more discussion of such examples.

(119)   a. Few politicians behave morally and are praised by their family members.
         b. Few politicians behave morally and few politicians are praised by their family members.

S-ATB constructions can also include examples like (120a), which has a different interpretation from the non-ATB construction in (120b). (120a) allows both the so-called internal reading and external reading of *same*, whereas (120b) allows the external reading of *same* only. The external reading of these two examples involves a covert comparison between a man referred to in the sentence and a man that is understood by the listener as having been already

---

[17] In each example of the noncoordinate constructions in (i), a paired reading seems to be allowed (Chaves 2021: 671). But my informants reject the examples. I thus do not discuss such examples.

(i)   a. Who$_{\{i, j\}}$ did the pictures of __$_i$ impress __$_j$ the most?
            (Possible answer: 'Robin's pictures impressed Sam the most.')
         b. Who$_{\{i, j\}}$ did the rivals of __$_i$ shoot __$_j$?
            (Possible answer: 'Robin's rivals shot Sam.')
         c. Who$_{\{i, j\}}$ did you send nude photos of __$_i$ to __$_j$?
            (Possible answer: 'I sent photos of Sam to Robin.')

contextually defined. The internal reading, by contrast, involves a comparison that is made available by the sentence itself. In (120a), the helping event and the ruining event are compared for the reading of *same*. No such a comparison is encoded in (120b). See Carlson (1987) for a discussion.

(120)   a. The same man, [Mary helped _] and [Jane ruined _].
         b. Mary helped the same man and Jane ruined the same man.

The right node raising version of the *same*-construction is addressed in Jackendoff (1977: 192) (e.g., *John whistled and Mary hummed the same tune*).

One possible syntactic analysis of an S-ATB construction is that the argument gap in each conjunct is an operator that moves to the left-edge of the clause, creating a derived predicate (the operation is called predicate abstraction in semantics); then the two derived predicates are coordinated, forming a coordinate predicate; and the left-edge expression is the argument (or subject) of this coordinate predicate (see Zhang 2014). For instance, (120a) has the basic structure in (121).

(121)   Few politicians [[Op_1 <Op_1> behave morally] [$_{J\text{-set}}$ and [Op_2 <Op_2> are praised <Op_2> by their family members]]]

In this structure, the first conjunct is a predicate derived by the raising of the Op_1 from a subject position. In the second conjunct, Op_2 is base-generated at the object position, moves to the subject position of the passive predicate, and then moves to the left-edge of the local clause, creating a derived predicate. Then, the two predicative conjuncts form a coordinate predicate. *Few politicians* is the argument of this coordinate predicate. Therefore, it and the gaps in the conjuncts are not copies created by any internal merge. The two different operators are both null. Therefore, we see gaps there.

In this non-unified analysis, the two major issues stated at the end of Section 5.1.1 are answered differently for different kinds of ATB constructions. In an I-ATB construction, the relation between the two gaps is that between a *proform* and its licensor, and the left-edge overt form and the gap in the first conjunct are two copies created by internal merge. In an R-ATB construction, the two gaps are repetitions, and the left-edge overt form and the gap in the first conjunct are two copies created by internal merge. Finally, in an S-ATB construction, the two gaps are two different null operators, and the left-edge overt form is an argument for a coordinate derived predicate. All three types of ATB constructions are derived without any coordination-specific syntactic operations.

5.1.3 Brief Comments on Other Analyses of Identical Across-the-Board Constructions

Among the three kinds of ATB constructions, only the I-ATB kind has been discussed in many studies. In this section, I briefly comment on other influential approaches to this construction: a forked movement approach, a sideward movement approach, and a multidominance approach.

The classic forked movement analysis of the indirect WH question in (122a) is (122b), where the elements in the two gap positions both move to the position of *who* (Williams 1977, 1978: 31; Blümel 2017).

(122)   a. who John saw and Bill hit
       b. who [[John saw t]$_s$ and [Bill hit t]]$_s$

Between the two gaps of an ATB construction, neither c-commands the other. If they form a movement chain, the movement mode is abnormal. The forked chain is claimed to exist in coordinate constructions only (Blümel 2017). Chomsky (2019: 46–47, 2021: 33–34) also assumes that the two gaps and the left-edge overt expression are copies of the same internal merge. Since the two gaps have no c-command relation, he states, "[so] crucially, the lack of c-command in coordination yields ATB" (Chomsky 2019: 47).

This forked internal merge analysis is obviously construction-specific, which can be avoided. The proform analysis introduced in the previous section indeed avoids such an ad hoc analysis.

In a sideward movement analysis (Nunes 2001; Hornstein & Nunes 2002), the shared element in an ATB construction first sideward moves from one conjunct, merging with an element in another working site. In the new working site, another conjunct is built. After the two conjuncts are integrated into a coordinate complex, the shared element finally moves out of the coordinate complex. In this analysis, (123a) is derived in the way illustrated in (123b).

(123)   a. Who does John like and Mary hate?
       b. [$_{CP}$ who does [John like <who>] and [Mary hate <who>]]

A multidominance analysis, proposed by Goodall (1987), Muadz (1991), and Moltmann (1992), among others, represents the semantic sharing of the two gaps in an ATB construction as the sharing of one daughter by two mothers (also see McCawley 1982), ignoring the extension condition, which states that a syntactic derivation can only be continued by applying operations to the root projection of the tree (Chomsky 1995). For example, as introduced in de Vries (2017: 32), (124b) is the structure of (124a), where *which book* is a sister of the two verbs, *like* and *hate*, and then moves to CP. In this structure, *which book* is a daughter shared by two VP mothers.

(124)   a. Which book does Peter like and Susan hate?

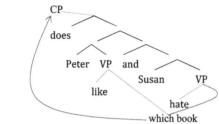

Compared to the proform analysis presented in the previous section, the sideward movement and the multidominance analyses are more complicated. I thus do not adopt them.

In this section, I have distinguished three kinds of ATB constructions and presented possible syntactic analyses. I have also shown why the simple proform analysis of the I-ATB construction introduced here is superior to other three analyses in the literature. Importantly, the analyses for all kinds of ATB constructions presented in Section 5.1.2 do not resort to any coordination-specific operations, unlike the classic and influential forked movement analysis.

5.2 From Nonconjuncts to Conjuncts: The Heterofunctional Coordination

Conjuncts are syntactic constituents. A syntactic element can move and then function as a conjunct; or conversely, a conjunct can move and then function as a nonconjunct element in the new position. In this (Section 5.2) and the next section (Section 5.3), we introduce these two situations, respectively.

Consider the coordinate examples in (125), which are called heterofunctional coordination (HFC) in Przepiórkowski (2022b). Przepiórkowski (2022b: 679) notes that the unlike conjuncts in HFCs must be generalized quantifiers, including wh-phrases and indefinites, excluding definite expressions such as proper names.

(125)   a. [Kada   i   gde]   si   ih   video?   [Serbo-Croatian]
              when   and where 2SG.AUX them saw
              'When and where did you see them?'   (Browne 1972: 223)
        b. [Nikto   i   nikomu]   ne pomogaet. [Russian]
              nobody.NOM and nobody.DAT NEG helps
              'Nobody helps anybody.'   (Mel'čuk 1988: 40)

The simplified structure of the HFC in (126a) is (126b) (based on Haida & Repp 2012):

(126)   a. Kto   i   kogo   videl?   [Russian]
            who   and   whom   saw
            'Who saw somebody and who was it?'
         b.

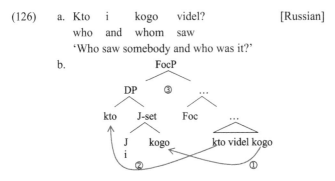

In (126b), the subject *kto* 'who' and the object *kogo* 'whom' each undergo a sideward movement to a different working site, forming a coordinate DP there. Then the DP is merged back to the structure in the old working site, forming a FocP. It is the sideward movement that makes each of the two nonconjunct elements to surface as a conjunct (Zhang 2007). See Haida and Repp's works for detailed argumentation of the analysis.

As pointed out by Bošković (2022a: 28), the coordination in a HFC is semantically expletive. Thus, the interpretation of (126a) is simply 'who saw whom,' and thus "there is no coordination of the wh-phrases in the interpretation of this construction." Thus, the coordinator in this use is a pure structure-builder, without any semantic function.

One important fact is that the order of the two conjuncts of a HFC follows the hierarchy in their base-positions. As in (126a), in (127a), the first conjunct comes from a subject position and the second one from an object position. In order to rule out the wrong order of the conjuncts in (127b), Bošković (2022a: 32) proposes that

> the relevant element needs to merge with the nonbase coordinator as soon as it is eligible for such merger. ... The result of this is that the order of elements in the derivationally formed ConjP will correspond to the order of these elements prior to derivational coordination formation, with ordering imposed on all conjuncts, not just on one relevant element (as it is with Superiority).

(127)   a.   Ko   i   šta   kupuje?   b.   *Šta i ko kupuje? [Serbo-Croatian]
              who and what buys

Heterofunctional coordinations have been studied by many (e.g., Whitman, 2002, 2004; Zhang 2007; Haida & Repp 2012; Citko & Gračanin-Yuksek 2013, Przepiórkowski 2022a, 2022b; Bošković 2022a: Appendix). Bošković

(2022b: 5, 10) further notes that the conjuncts in the construction cannot move from different clauses.

Some other constructions that look like HFCs have been shown to have structures different from those of HFCs. Citko and Gračanin-Yuksek (2020) argue that unlike the Russian HFC in (126a), the English WH coordinate construction such as (128a) underlyingly involves coordination of two interrogative CPs with a single fronted wh-phrase and an elided TP in each CP. Moreover, Zyman (2020) argues that the English in situ WH coordinate construction such as (128b) is derived by VP-coordination, where the verbs have an ATB dependency. Therefore, such constructions are not derived by the movement of an element to a conjunct position.

(128) a. What and where has John eaten (in the last five years)?   (Grosu 1987: 428)
       b. Mary ate what and when to impress Sue?!   (Zyman 2020: 1)

The coordination of the generalized quantifiers discussed in this subsection indicates that conjuncts can be internally merged from other syntactic positions, in a normal way. There is no construction-specific rule in forming a coordinate complex.

5.3 From Conjuncts to Nonconjuncts: The Split Argument Construction

A conjunct may move and then surface as a nonconjunct element. In this section, I introduce such a possible derivation of a split argument construction, and then compare the derivation with the derivation of a comitative construction. A comitative marker such as the English *with* occurs in the latter, but not in the former. The derivations of the two constructions do not need any coordination-specific operations.

5.3.1 Deriving Split Argument Constructions via Conjunct Raising

The split argument construction (SAC) refers to sentences like those in (129), where the preverbal and postverbal arguments share the same thematic relation with the verb. Each of the two SACs has a counterpart in (130), where a coordinate complex containing the two nominals functions as a single argument and theta-role bearer for the same verb. In English, the coordinate DP complex in the non-SAC variant occurs in a subject position, as seen in (130).

(129) a. John married Jane. b. Italy borders France.

(130) a. [John and Jane] married. b. [Italy and France] border.

In addition to *marry* and *border*, other collective verbs such as *date*, *divorce*, *hug*, *fight*, and *meet* may also occur in SACs (Levin 1993: 36–37). Parallel examples can also be found in other languages such as German (Zhang 2010: 142).

A SAC encodes a single eventuality, and thus the predicate may not be distributive. The distributive adverb *separately* is rejected in (131a), and the intrinsically distributive verb *sneeze* is also rejected in (131b).

(131)   a. *John married Jane separately.   (cf. (129a))
         b. *John sneezed Mary.
             Intended: 'John and Mary sneezed.'

Zhang (2010: 144) uses four arguments to claim that the two DPs of a SAC are conjuncts of a coordinate DP in their base-positions. First, collective verbs such as *marry* and *fight* in English require their argument to be plural. In a SAC, if the two singular DPs form a coordinate complex in their base positions, the requirement of the collective verb is satisfied. Second, if the two nominals of a SAC form a complex in their base positions, and the complex has a unique theta relation with the verb, the verb will not license two identical theta roles. Third, if the two nominals form a coordinate complex in their base positions, the alternation between a SAC and a coordinate construction, as seen between (129) and (130), will not deviate from the uniformity of theta-assignment hypothesis (UTAH).[18] Fourth, the two DPs in a SAC may exchange their positions without affecting the truth value of the proposition, and this possibility is also seen in a symmetrical coordinate construction (cf. (11)). In such a coordinate construction, either conjunct may be merged with a (null) coordinator first.

If the two DPs of a SAC form a coordinate complex in their base-positions, a SAC is derived by the raising of the first conjunct. For example, the simplified structure of (129a) is (132), where $\oslash$ is a null coordinator (i.e., J is not lexically realized).

(132)   [$_{IP}$ John$_i$ married [$_{DP}$ t$_i$ [$_{J\text{-set}}$ $\oslash$ [$_{DP}$ Jane]]] …]

Zhang (2010: 147–153) argues that the preverbal DP of a SAC exhibits the syntactic properties of nominals that have undergone an internal merge, supporting the conjunct raising hypothesis.

Note that the information structure status of the raised conjunct in a SAC is different from its correlated DP in a non-SAC variant, where the DP remains in

---

[18] Uniformity of theta-assignment hypothesis (Baker 1997) states that identical thematic relation ships between items are represented by identical structural relationships between the items before any internal merge occurs.

the DP-complex. Internal Merge is associated with discourse-informational meaning (Chomsky 2022). One cannot use the information structure difference to argue against any movement analysis, including the conjunct raising analysis.

Moreover, an agent-oriented adverb is associated with a raised agent only. In the SAC in (133a), *Bill* is raised but *Kim* is not. In the coordinate construction in (133b), both DPs are in the raised complex. Therefore, Kim does not have to be careful/intentional in (133a), but must be so in (133b).

(133)   a. Bill {carefully/intentionally} hugged Kim.
            b. Bill and Kim {carefully/intentionally} hugged.

In this analysis, a SAC is derived by the movement of a conjunct from a coordinate DP that has a null coordinator. The preverbal DP may occur wherever a language permits an argument to move to, and the postverbal DP remains in the coordinate complex. It is the coordinate complex that has a unique theta relation with the verb.

In Section 4.2.1, we have seen that conjunct movement is possible in some languages, indicating that the CC is not a universal constraint on syntactic operations. We now see that SACs can be derived by conjunct movement. Also, the function change from a conjunct to a nonconjunct contrasts with the function change from a nonconjunct to a conjunct in the derivation of a HFC (Section 5.2). In the formation of both constructions, no construction-specific operation is needed.

5.3.2 A Comparison with the Derivation of Comitatives

In English, a *with*-phrase can be associated with a verbal or nominal phrase. In the former case, it introduces either a manner or an instrument, as seen in (134a) and (134b), respectively. But if the DP in a *with*-phrase is associated with a DP of the same semantic type (e.g., both are human), it is called a comitative. In (134c), *with Mary* is associated with *John*, while in (134d), *with the milk* is associated with *the beer*. In (134e), *a hat on the head* is not a human and *she*, the only other nominal in the example, is human. Thus, the *with*-phrase is not a comitative (see Trembly 1996 for an analysis).

(134)   a. John ate the dinner with good cheer.
            b. Max eats with chopsticks.
            c. John drank beer with Mary.
            d. Robin compared the beer with the milk.
            e. She was walking with a hat on the head.

We have shown that in a SAC, one DP is moved from a coordinate complex. Kayne (1994: 64) and Zhang (2007) argue that in an English comitative construction (ComC), if a *with*-phrase and its associated DP are not next to each other, the latter is also moved from a complex DP, although this complex DP is not a coordinate one. Thus, a simplified structure of (134c) is (135).

(135)   [$_{IP}$ John$_i$ drank beer [$_{DP}$ t$_i$ with Mary] . . .]

In this subsection, I briefly compare a SAC and a ComC.

Similarities between a SAC and a ComC include the following. First, like a SAC, a ComC encodes a single eventuality, and thus no distributive marker such as *separately* or *both* is allowed (Kayne 1994: 66).

(136)   a. Tony and Geezer both lifted the amp.
          b. #Tony both lifted the amp with Geezer.   (Williams 2015: 175) (cf. (131))

Second, *together* cannot occur with either a SAC or a symmetrical ComC, as well as an argument of a collective predicate, as seen in (137a), (137b), and (137c), respectively. If (137c) indicates that *together* is incompatible with an obligatorily collective predication (cf. (137d)), (137a), and (137b) show that they share this collectiveness.

(137)   a. *John married Mary together.
          b. *John lifted the amp with Mary together.   (Williams 2015: 175)
          c. *John and Mary together are married.   (Moltmann 2004: 292)
          d. Together, Tony and Geezer lifted the amp.

Third, like a SAC, a ComC also rejects a reciprocal in English, a fact noted by Baker (1992: 46), as seen in (138) and (139b).

(138)   *John met Mary each other.   (SAC; Zhang 2010: 152)

(139)   a. John and Mary kissed each other.
          b. *John kissed each other with Mary.

Fourth, as in a SAC, an agent-oriented adverb in a ComC is associated with a raised agent DP only; therefore, Geezer does not have to be careful/intentional in (140a), but must be so in (140b).

(140)   a. Tony {carefully/intentionally} lifted the amp with Geezer.
          b. Tony and Geezer {carefully/intentionally} lifted the amp.

Fifth, some arguments for the raising of a DP from a complex nominal in a SAC also apply to a ComC where one DP is separated from its associated DP. For example, in such a ComC, the preverbal DP and the postverbal DP have the same theta relation with the verb: either both are agent or both are theme (Lakoff & Peters 1969: 120; see Zhang 2007: 141). Thus, comitative is not an independent theta role (see Tremblay 1996: 81).

Zhang (2007) distinguishes symmetrical and asymmetrical ComCs (see Özay-Demircioğlu 2021 for an experimental contrast between the two types of ComCs). (134c) and (134d) are both symmetrical ComCs, but (141) is an asymmetrical ComC (Zhang 2007: 146). Unlike a symmetrical ComC, the DP in the *with*-phrase in an asymmetrical ComC denotes an appurtenance of the referent of the other DP. However, in neither construction, the two DPs may have different theta roles. "Comitatives are always interpreted in relation to direct arguments (internal, external). There are no oblique oriented comitatives" (Franco & Manzini 2017: 14). In both types of ComC, the separation of the two DPs is derived by the raising of the first DP from a DP complex. It is the complex DP that has a unique thematic relation with the verb, as in a SAC.

(141)   John will drink beer with Bill by his side.

One difference between a SAC and a symmetrical ComC in English is that a complex DP is base-generated as an external argument in a SAC, but the complex DP can be either an external or internal argument of a verb in a ComC. Accordingly, either an external or internal argument can split in a ComC, deriving an external argument ComC, such as (134c), or internal argument ComC, such as (142). See Zhang (2007) for the derivation details of the different types of ComCs.

(142)   The beer was mixed with the milk.

We can see the basic similarities and contrasts among the three constructions in (143).

(143)   a. [IP John$_i$ married [DP t$_i$ [J-set $\oslash$ [DP Jane]]] ...]   (SAC)
         b. [IP John$_i$ drank beer [DP t$_i$ with Mary] ...]   (symmetrical ComC)
         c. [IP John$_i$ will drink beer [DP t$_i$ [PP with Bill by his side]] ...] (asymmetrical ComC)

Another difference between a SAC and a ComC is the presence of a comitative marker, such as the English *with*. In Zhang (2007; cf. Kayne 1994: 64), *with* is a D in a symmetrical ComC, but is a P in an asymmetrical ComP. In a SAC, however, it is a null coordinator that links the two DPs. Neither the D nor the P use of *with* is a coordinator, which has no category feature. Thus, unlike *and*, *with* can be stranded (*Who did you go with*; **Who did you go and*), and its combination with the DP to its right can move (*With who did you go there*; **And who did you go there*). Also, parallel DPs can each follow an *and*, as seen in (72b), but parallel DPs cannot each follow a *with* (e.g., **Tom with Dick with Harry*). In the J-theory, *with* is not a J element, since it has categorial features.

In many languages, comitatives and coordinate constructions are closely related (e.g., Stolz et al. 2006: 21). In Mandarin *gen* 'and, with' and *he* 'and, with' are used either as conjunctions or comitative markers.

In this section, I have discussed the derivation of a SAC, such as (144a), comparing the derivation with that of a ComC such as (144b) and (144c). I have claimed that in all of these constructions, the preverbal DP is raised from a complex DP, but the complex DP is a coordinate one for a SAC.

(144)   a. John met Jane in the street.   (SAC)
        b. John drank beer with Jane.   (external argument ComC)
        c. The beer was mixed with the milk.   (internal argument ComC)

Unlike the other constructions discussed in this section, no coordinator occurs in a SAC. But a SAC can be derived from a coordinate construction where the position of a coordinator is null. It is conjunct movement that derives a SAC. One can see how the null J theory and conjunct movement are able to explain the derivation of the construction. Thus, like other syntactic constituents, a conjunct can move (also see Section 4.2.1).

5.4 From Conjuncts to Parts of Conjuncts: The Modifier-Sharing Construction

Dependencies can be established between two coordinate complexes. Conjuncts in one coordinate complex can move and then surface as parts of conjuncts in another complex, or vice versa. In this (Section 5.4) and the next section (Section 5.5), we introduce these two situations, respectively. Both constructions show that conjuncts behave like other syntactic constituents.

Consider a construction such as (145) (Perlmutter and Ross 1970). In this example, the relative clause (RC) seems to be shared by two modified elements, or called Heads, namely, *a man* and *a woman*.[19] The two Heads are distributed in the two matrix clauses respectively. Zhang (2007, 2010) calls the construction modifier-sharing construction (MSC).

(145)   Mary met a man$_i$ and John met a woman$_j$ [who$_{i\&j}$ knew each other$_{i\&j}$ well].

---

[19] I use "Head" to refer to the nominal modified by a RC, such as *man* in *the man who came*. Such a nominal is also called antecedent or "Head nominal." The term "head" is reserved for the element that has a complement in a syntactic structure.

(145) cannot be derived by extraposition as in (146a) or by deletion as in (146b). The extraposition is not possible because the RC in the gap position $\_k$ is ill-formed semantically, given that *each other* is not licensed by any c-commanding plural element there. As claimed by Gazdar (1981: 179), the RC in an MSC "must be generated in situ." The deletion in (146b) is not possible for a similar reason. This indicates that the RC must be semantically related to the two Heads simultaneously.

(146)   a. *Mary met a man$_i$ $\_k$ and John met a woman$_j$ [who knew each other well]$_k$.
        b. *Mary met a man$_i$ [~~who knew each other well~~] and John met a woman$_j$ [who knew each other well].

The two Heads of the RC in an MSC must play parallel roles. In the unacceptable (147), one Head is a subject and the other is an object.

(147)   *A man entered the room and I saw a woman who were   (Baltin 2006: 255) similar.

An RC can modify a coordinate nominal, as seen in (148) (Vergnaud 1974: 81ff.; Jackendoff 1977: 190; among others). Such a construction is called Hydra. A Hydra is different from an MSC in that the antecedent is not "split" into two clauses.

(148)   [$_{DP}$ [$_{DP}$ a man$_i$ and a woman$_j$]$_m$ [$_{RC}$ who$_m$ knew each other well]]

Showing systematic syntactic similarities between Hydras and MSCs, Zhang (2010: §6.3) finds that in both constructions the RC takes a single coordinate DP complex as its Head, and thus the RC is not syntactically multiply-Headed. The two constructions show the following similarities. First, the RCs in both a Hydra and an MSC are restrictive, and thus both constructions reject pronouns or proper names as their Heads.

(149)   a. *Mary met {him/Bill}$_i$ and John met [a woman]$_j$ [who$_{i\&j}$ knew each other well].
        b. *{he/Bill}$_i$ and [a woman]$_j$ [who$_{i\&j}$ knew each other well]

Also, in English, a restrictive RC may be introduced by *that*, but a nonrestrictive one cannot. The RC in a MSC can also be introduced by *that*, patterning with a restrictive RC.[20]

---

[20] Cinque (2019: 77) gives the following example to show that, in certain cases, *that* is not allowed in a MSC:

(i)   A man$_i$ entered the room and a woman$_j$ went out {who/?*that}$_{i+j}$ were quite similar.

(150)   Tom bought a can opener and Alice bought a dictionary [that were once
         owned by Leonard Bloomfield].   (McCawley 1982: 100)

Second, both Hydras and MSCs license reciprocals, which need a plural
antecedent. We have seen this in (148) and (145), respectively. If the derivation
of the MSC in (145) is similar to that of the Hydra in (148), in which the two
singular nominals form a coordinate complex, the licensing of the reciprocal is
explained.

Third, the modifier in a Hydra does not have to be a RC, and this is also
true of an MSC. The modifier in the Hydra in (151a) is a PP, and the modifier
in the SMC in (151b) is also a PP. Also see Bobaljik (2017) for a study of
adjectival Hydras: two DP conjuncts share the same adjective modifier in
some languages.

(151)   a. the boy and the girl [with a common background]   (Jackendoff 1977: 191)
         b. Fred bought a book and Mary got a magazine [about exactly the same topic]
                                                          (Chaves 2014: 854)

Fourth, Vergnaud (1974: 90) notes that the determiners of the Head nominals
must be identical in Hydras, and Moltmann (1992: §2.4.5) further notes that this
property is shared by MSCs:

(152)   a. *a man and the woman who knew each other well   (Hydra)
         b. *John saw the man and Mary saw a woman who knew each other well. (MSC)

In (152a), *a man and the woman* is modified by the RC *who knew each other
well*. Since the determiners *a* and *the* are not identical, and a nominal with
contrastive D properties cannot be modified by the same RC, the Hydra is not
acceptable. Parallel to this, in (152b), the two antecedents are *a man* and *the
woman*, and again the difference in determiners causes the MSC to be unacceptable. The account for the restriction on Hydras applies to MSCs, if the former is
a step to derive the latter (see Moltmann 1992: §2.4.5 and Fox & Johnson 2016
for discussions). See Fox and Johnson (2016) for more types of Ds that are
shared by the split antecedents in MSCs.

We thus claim that the antecedent of the relative pronoun in an MSC is a
coordinate complex with a null conjunction. We propose that MSCs are
derived by the sideward movement of the conjuncts from this modified
DP. Each conjunct is selected by a verb. The two nominals take part in the
building of a coordinate clausal complex. Finally, the complex nominal in
the old working site is merged with the whole construction. The structure
of (145) is (153).

(153)

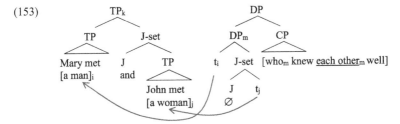

In this analysis, DP_i and DP_j form a coordinate complex with a null J (a null coordinator) in their base-positions (cf. Cecchetto & Donati 2015: 75). Then, "why is only one *and* pronounced (that of the CPs) and the second (of DPs) not pronounced?" (McKinney-Bock 2013: 116). My answer is that if the second conjunct, as well as the first one, is moved, there is nothing to support the proclitic *and* morphologically (see (54b)). Thus, the coordinator in DP_m is null.

We now compare our analysis with Moltmann (1992) and Wilder's (2008: 253) multidominance analysis of MSCs. In Wilder (1999), the structure of (145) is (154). In this analysis, the apparent antecedents do not move. Instead, they are linked to the RC by special tree branches.

(154)

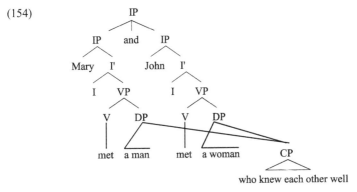

In addition to the linearization complexity (see de Vries 2017: 33), another disadvantage of this analysis is that the two antecedents of the relative pronoun, *a man* and *a woman* in (154), never form a constituent in the derivation, and thus the shared properties of MSCs and Hydras seem to be accidental. Moltmann (1992: Ch. 2) claims that, in an MSC, the two shared nominals are implicitly coordinated, but they never form a constituent. This differs from (153), where two nominals are conjoined by a null conjunction at a certain step of the derivation. If the two nominals are selected by two verbs respectively, they need not have the same D-features. The multidominance analysis must stipulate certain constraints to restrict the derivations, in order to explain (152b). In (153), the restriction is captured naturally: it is the same restriction seen on Hydras, and the structure of a Hydra is an early step of the derivation to form an MSC.

In this section, I have proposed a syntactic derivation for MSCs such as *Mary met a man and John met a woman who knew each other well*. I have claimed that the two modified elements of an MSC are originally two conjuncts of a coordinate nominal. Then each undergoes sideward movement to a new working site, where it is selected by a verb. Thus, an MSC has two coordinate complexes, although only one coordinator surfaces. Again, conjuncts can move. This is compatible with the conclusion reached in Section 4.2.1.

5.5 From Parts of Conjuncts to Conjuncts: The Interwoven Dependency Construction

One more coordinate construction can be derived by normal syntactic operations. In this section, I introduce a high coordinate complex whose two conjuncts are associated with the gaps in the two conjuncts of a low coordinate complex, respectively. Two examples are in (155). In (155a), for example, in the left-edge coordinate complex, the first conjunct *which nurse* is related to the object gap of verb *date* in the first clausal conjunct, and the second conjunct *which hostess* is related to the object gap of the verb *marry* in the second clausal conjunct.

(155)   a. [[Which nurse]$_i$ and [which hostess]$_j$]$_k$ did Fred date   (Postal 1998: 134)
            _$_i$ and Bob marry _$_j$, respectively?
         b. [The dogs and the roosters]$_k$ barked and crowed all   (Zhang 2010: 170)
            night.

The dependencies in such a construction are called interwoven dependencies in Postal (1998: 134). Zhang (2010) thus calls the construction interwoven dependency construction (IDC). Interwoven dependency constructions have been discussed in Tai (1969: 14), Dougherty (1970), Postal (1998), and Bošković (2022a). See Zhang (2010: 171–172) for a brief review of old analyses of the construction. In Zhang's (2010: §6.4) analysis, the two conjuncts of the high coordinate complex are moved from the two gap positions of the low coordinate complex, respectively, by sideward movement. The two nominal movement dependencies exhibit island effects (Bošković 2022a). I update my analysis of the basic derivation structure of (156a) in (156b); and that of (157a) in (157b).

(156)

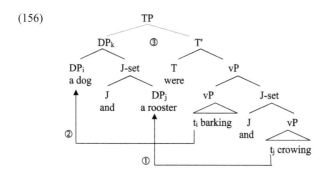

(157) a. Which nurse and which hostess did Fred date and Bob marry, respectively?

b.

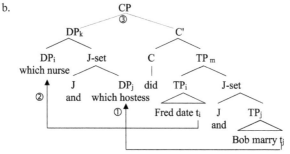

The timing of the sideward movement, and the timing of the merger of the high coordinate complex into the structure are important (Zhang 2010: 174; Bošković 2022a). For the A-dependency type of IDC, as in (156b), it is the high coordinate complex, rather than the subject inside a clausal conjunct alone, that is probed by T (triggering the plural agreement *were,* not *was,* in (156), for example).

Zhang's analysis is refined and extended in Bošković (2022a). First, in addition to the A-dependencies in examples like (156a) and the A-bar dependencies in examples like (157a), Bošković (2022a) shows that APs can also be extracted to build an IDC in languages that allow such extraction, as seen in (158). But he also reports that, so far, no head dependencies have been found in IDCs. The example in (159) shows that head dependencies in the English IDC is not acceptable, although head coordination is possible (e.g., (93c)).

(158) Crvene i   bijele ona suknje i   kapute prodaje.   [Serbo-Croatian]
       red   and white she skirts   and coats is.selling
       'She is selling red skirts and white coats.'

(159) *Will$_i$, can$_j$, and must$_k$ [John t$_i$ buy a book], [Peter t$_j$ sell a magazine], and [Mary t$_k$ borrow a novel] respectively?   (Bošković 2022a: 13)

Second, Bošković points out that the high coordination in an IDC is semantically expletive, as in a HFC (see our Section 5.2). He further notes that in an IDC, "as a result only the most neutral coordinator is used in such coordination (even when a different element is used in the lower position)." In English, *and*, instead of *or* and *but*, occurs in the high coordinate complex in an IDC, as shown in (160) (Bošković 2022a: 16). Note that if *there* is used as a locative proform, it contrasts with *here*; but if it is used as an expletive, it has no other parallel forms. Similarly, the expletive *and* cannot be replaced with another coordinator.

(160)   a. Which book **and** which magazine did John buy **or** Mary sell respectively?
         b. *Which book **or** which magazine did John buy or Mary sell respectively?

The derivation of an IDC contains a step that is similar to the derivation of a HFC, that is, a new coordinate complex is built directly by sideward movement of some elements. But, unlike a HFC, the elements that undergo sideward movement can be definite, as seen in (155b), and can be long-distance, as seen in (161).

(161)   Which writer$_i$ and which actor$_j$ does John adore t$_i$ and Peter claim t$_j$ will succeed in Hollywood respectively?

                                                            (Bošković 2022a: 4)

Since an IDC always allows a distributive adverb such as *respectively*, it is distributive exclusively.[21] Also, there is no nonexhaustive IDC, as shown in (162b) (also see Bošković 2022a: 3), unlike the nonexhaustive ATB construction in (163).

(162)   a. Which book$_i$, which magazine$_j$ and which novel$_k$ did [John buy t$_i$], [Bill read t$_j$] and [Mary borrow t$_k$] respectively?

                                                            (Bošković 2022a: 3)
         b. *[Which book$_i$ and which magazine$_j$] did [John buy t$_i$], [Bill rent a DVD] and [Mary borrow t$_k$] (respectively)?

(163)   How many courses can you take _ for credit, still stay sane, and get all A's in _?
         (= (115))

In an IDC, different elements are moved from different conjuncts. The possible derivation indicates that like other kinds of syntactic constituents, a

---

[21] The adverb *respectively* is not coordination-specific (Munn 1993: 9), as seen in (i) (Chavis 2012: 301).

(i)   The following two sections will deal with these two issues, respectively.

Thus, the occurrence of *respectively* does not motivate the coordination-specific operation Form-Sequence (Chomsky 2019: 50, 2021: 31).

conjunct can also host a lower copy of an internal merge. This is compatible with the conclusion reached in Section 4.2.2.

5.6 Summary

In this section, I have introduced the derivations of five coordinate constructions: ATB, HFC, SAC (comparing with ComC), MSC, and IDC. In the derivations, there is no forked movement chain, conjuncts may move, and elements may also move from conjuncts. Again, there is no coordinate construction-specific syntax.

6 Conclusions and Theoretical Considerations

In this Element, I have discussed the syntactic relation between conjuncts, the syntactic properties of conjuncts, the morpho-syntactic properties of coordinators, and the merge and move operations in deriving five coordinate constructions (ATB, HFC, SAC, MSC, and IDC).

The following major issues have been clarified: there is no coordinate construction-specific functional head (e.g., Co, Conj, &, Boolean, as proposed in some studies in the literatures), structural representation, or syntactic operation. I conclude that the syntax of coordination and that of modification can be unified. Specifically, they both use the categoryless functional element J. J is realized by a coordinator or a modification marker. These two kinds of functional elements share systematic formal properties. Moreover, both coordinate and modification constructions are built via two basic levels of merger (i.e., J takes either a modifier or a low conjunct as its complement; and the result is merged with a categorizer, which is either the modified element or the other conjunct), as shown in the two trees in (164).

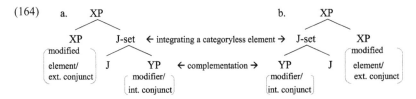

Furthermore, if a left clausal conjunct has an adverbial reading, it is in the same syntactic position as a left adverbial clause (i.e., the complement of J); otherwise, it can be the sister of a J-set. Thus, the surface linear order alone does not decide the syntactic position of a conjunct. Accordingly, a J-set can either follow or precede its categorizer, XP, as shown in (164a) and (164b), respectively.

Whether a construction has a modification or conjunctive reading is not decided by the two levels of merger in (164). Instead, it depends on two factors. One is the semantic relation between J's complement (YP) and J-set's categorizer (XP), and the other is the lexical properties of the element that realizes J. This is summarized in (165) (the numbers in the brackets are the labels of the relevant examples).

(165)   Representing conjunctive and modifying readings, with examples

relation J	XP and YP are semantically symmetrical	XP and YP are semantically asymmetrical
overt &-marker	Conjunctive: (11); Expletive in IDC: (155)	Modifying: (30); Expletive in HFC: (126)
overt Mod marker		Modifying: (79)
⊘	Conjunctive: (57)	Conjunctive: (22) with reading B; Modifying: (22) with reading A, (80)
er in Cl. Chinese	Conjunctive: (85a)	Modifying: (85b)

From the table in (165), we can see that if XP and YP are semantically symmetrical, they may form a construction that has a conjunctive reading, regardless of whether an overt coordinator occurs or not. However, if they are not semantically symmetrical, they may form a construction that has a conjunctive reading, or a construction that has a modifying reading, even in the presence of an overt coordinator. Also, an overt coordinator may be used as an expletive in HFCs and IDCs; and the same formative, such as the Classical Chinese *er*, may be used as a joining marker or modification marker. The meaning instability of an overt coordinator, or J element in general, follows Carlson's (2000) generalization that functional elements often present mismatches in form and interpretation that lexical elements do not.

The major contributions of this Element include the recognition of a categoryless functional element and the unification of the syntax of coordination and modification. One further theoretical remark is that the syntactic representations of argument-taking relation and other syntactic relations can be distinguished by the presence of the categoryless J: J does not occur in the argument-taking relation, but it occurs in other syntactic relations. J introduces a nonargument element to X. It is the feature makeup of a functional element, rather than any special type of representation or operation, that explains the differences between the argument-taking relation and nonargument taking relation in syntax. We have thus reached a new understanding of the syntax of building modification and nonmodification constructions (also see Safir 2022). The concept construction is not primitive. Instead, each construction comes from a specific feature makeup of certain functional elements.

With respect to coordination, as shown in many other studies (e.g., Kehler 2002; Zhang 2010; Oda 2021; Altshuler & Truswell 2022), the CSC is not a purely syntactic constraint. With respect to modification, we need to reconsider the nature of the XP-YP combination. It has been assumed that in addition to standard formulation of Merge, which creates unordered sets (called Set-Merge), another kind of merge is needed to capture the asymmetry between a modifier and the modified expression, which generates ordered sets (called Pair-Merge) (see Rubin 2003 and Safir 2022). As demonstrated in this Element, the asymmetry in a modification relation can be accounted for by the standard formulation of Merge, and therefore does not require Pair-Merge. If one expression is a modifier of the other expression, it is a categoryless J-set, and consequently, it must be the other expression to label the structure.

I expect these new insights to serve as a springboard to further research on coordinate structures and syntactic theories.

References

Abbott, Barbara. 1976. Right node raising as a test for constituenthood. *Linguistic Inquiry* 7.4: 639–642.

Adger, David. 2013. *A syntax of substance*. MIT Press.

Agbayani, Brian, Chris Golston, and Dasha Henderer. 2011. Prosodic movement. In Mary Byram Washburn, Katherine McKinney-Bock, Erika Varis, Ann Sawyer, and Barbara Tomaszewicz (eds.), *Proceedings of the 28th West Conference on Formal Linguistics*, 231–239. Somerville, MA: Cascadilla Proceedings Project.

Aldridge, Edith. 2017. Internally and externally headed relative clauses in Tagalog. *Glossa: A Journal of General Linguistics* 2.1: 41. 1–33, DOI: https://doi.org/10.5334/gjgl.175.

Altshuler, Daniel and Robert Truswell. 2022. *Coordination and the syntax–discourse interface*. Oxford University Press.

Baker, Mark. 1992. Unmatched chains and the representation of plural pronouns. *Natural Language Semantics* 1: 33–73.

Baker, Mark. 1997. Thematic roles and syntactic structure. In L. Haegeman (ed.), *Elements of grammar*, 73–137. Dordrecht: Kluwer Academic Publishers.

Baltin, Mark. 2006. Extraposition. In M. Everaert and H. van Riemsdijk (eds.), *The Blackwell companion to syntax*. 237–271. Oxford: Blackwell.

Barotto, Alessandra, and Caterina Mauri. 2022. Non-exhaustive connectives. *STUF-Language Typology and Universals* 75.2: 317–377.

Bloomfield, Leonard. 1933. *Language*. New York: Holt, Rinehart & Winston.

Blümel, Andreas. 2017. *Symmetry, shared labels and movement in syntax*. Berlin: Walter de Gruyter.

Blümel, Rudolf. 1914. *Einführung in die Syntax*. Heidelberg: C. Winter.

Bobaljik, Jonathan. 2017. Adjectival hydras: Restrictive modifiers above DP? In Clemens Mayr and Edwin Williams (eds.), *Wiener Linguistische Gazette (WLG)* 82: 13–22.

Borer, Hagit. 2005. *In name only*. Oxford University Press.

Borsley, Robert D. 1994. In defense of coordinate structures. *Linguistic Analysis* 24: 218–246.

Borsley, Robert D. 2005. Against ConjP. *Lingua* 115.4: 461–482.

Bošković, Željko. 2020a. On the coordinate structure constraint and the adjunct condition. In András Bárány, Theresa Biberauer, Jamie Douglas and Sten Vikner (eds.), *Syntactic architecture and its consequences II: Between syntax and morphology*, 227–258. Berlin: Language Science Press.

Bošković, Željko. 2020b. On the coordinate structure constraint, across-the-board-movement, phases, and labeling. In Jeroen van Craenenbroeck, Cora Pots, and Tanja Temmerman (eds.), *Recent Developments in Phase Theory*. Berlin: De Gruyter Mouton. 133–182.

Bošković, Željko. 2022a. On the limit of across-the-board movement: Distributed extraction coordination. *Philosophies*, 7.10. https://doi.org/10.3390/philosophies7010010.

Bošković, Željko. 2022b. Wh&wh coordinations. lingbuzz/006842.

Bresnan, Joan and Höskuldur Thráinsson 1990. A note on Icelandic coordination. In Joan Mailing and Annie Zaenen (eds.), *Syntax and semantics 24: Modern Icelandic syntax*, 355–365. San Diego: Academic Press

Browne, III, E. Wayles. 1972. Conjoined question words and a limitation of English surface structures. *Linguistic Inquiry* 3.2: 223–226.

Bruening, Benjamin. 2014. Precede-and-command revisited. *Language* 90.2: 342–388.

Bruening, Benjamin. 2022. Selectional violation in coordination (a response to Patejuk and Przepiórkowski to appear). *Linguistic Inquiry*, to appear.

Bruening, Benjamin and Eman Al Khalaf. 2020. Category mismatches in coordination revisited. *Linguistic Inquiry* 51.1: 1–36.

Büring, Daniel and Katharina Hartmann. 2015. Semantic coordination without syntactic coordinators. In Ida Toivonen, Piroska Csúri, and Emile Van Der Zee (eds.), *Structures in the mind: Essays on language, music, and cognition in honor of Ray Jackendoff*, 41–61. Cambridge, MA: MIT Press.

Carlson, Greg. 1983. Marking constituents. In Frank Heny and Barry Richards (eds.), *Linguistic categories: Auxiliaries and related puzzles. Vol. I: Categories*. 49–68. Dordrecht: Reidel.

Carlson, Greg. 1987. Same and different: Some consequences for syntax and semantics. *Linguistics and Philosophy* 10: 531–565.

Carlson, Greg. 2000. "Mismatches" of form and interpretation. *University of Rochester Working Papers in the Language Sciences*, Spring, no. 1: 97–106.

Cecchetto, Carlo and Caterina Donati. 2015. *(Re)labeling*. Cambridge, MA: MIT Press.

Chaves, Rui P. 2012. Conjunction, cumulation and respectively readings. *Journal of Linguistics* 48.2: 297–344.

Chaves, Rui P. 2014. On the disunity of right-node raising phenomena: Extraposition, ellipsis, and deletion. *Language* 90.4: 834–886.

Chaves, Rui P. 2021. Island phenomena and related matters. In Stefan Müller, Anne Abeillé, Robert D. Borsley and Jean- Pierre Koenig (eds.), *Head-driven phrase structure grammar: The handbook*, 665–723. Berlin: Language Science Press.

Chomsky, Noam. 1957. *Syntactic structures*. The Hague: Mouton and Co.

Chomsky, Noam. 1965. *Aspects of the theory of syntax*. Cambridge, MA: MIT Press.

Chomsky, Noam. 1981. *Lectures on government and binding*. Dordrecht: Foris.

Chomsky, Noam. 1995. *The minimalist program*. Cambridge, MA: MIT Press, 1–67.

Chomsky, Noam. 2002. *On nature and language*. Cambridge: Cambridge University Press.

Chomsky, Noam. 2013. Problems of projection. *Lingua* 130: 33–49.

Chomsky, Noam. 2019. UCLA Lectures. Invited lectures at the Department of Linguistics, University of California, Los Angeles, April 29–30, May 1–2, 2019. Manuscript available with some changes and an introduction by Robert Freidin. https://ling.auf.net/lingbuzz/005485.

Chomsky, Noam. 2021. Minimalism: Where are we now, and where can we hope to go. *Gengo Kenkyu* 160: 1–40.

Chomsky, Noam. 2022. Genuine explanation. Manuscript, University of Arizona and MIT.

Chomsky, Noam and George Miller. 1963. Introduction to the formal analysis of natural languages. In R. D. Luce, R. Bush, and E. Galanter (eds.), *Handbook of mathematical psychology*, vol. 2, 269–322. Wiley.

Chung, Sandra. 1991. Functional heads and proper government in Chamorro. *Lingua* 85: 85–134.

Cinque, Guglielmo. 2019. A note on relative clauses with split antecedents. In Metin Bağrıaçık, Anne Breitbarth, and Karen De Clercq (eds.) *Mapping linguistic data*: *Essays in honour of Liliane Haegeman*, 75–81. https://biblio.ugent.be/publication/8625919/file/8625920#page=75.

Citko, Barbara and Martina Gračanin-Yuksek. 2013. Towards a new typology of coordinated wh-questions. *Journal of Linguistics* 49: 1–32.

Citko, Barbara and Martina Gračanin-Yuksek. 2020. Conjunction saves multiple sluicing: How*(and) why? *Glossa: A Journal of General Linguistics* 5.1: 92. 1–29. DOI: https://doi.org/10.5334/gjgl.1112

Collins, Chris. 1997. *Local economy*. Cambridge: MIT Press.

Collins, Chris. 2022. The complexity of trees, universal grammar and economy conditions. *Biolinguistics*, 16.e9573, https://doi.org/10.5964/bioling.9573

Culicover, Peter and Ray Jackendoff. 1997. Semantic subordination despite syntactic coordination. *Linguistic Inquiry* 28.2: 195–217.

Davies, William. 2000. Events in Madurese reciprocals. *Oceanic Linguistics* 39.1: 123–143.

Déchaine, Rose-Marie. 2005. Grammar at the borderline: A case study of P as a lexical category. In John Alderete et al. (eds.), *Proceedings of the 24th West*

Coast Conference on Formal Linguistics, 1–18. Somerville, MA: Cascadilla Proceedings Project.

Dik, Simon. 1968. *Coordination: Its implications for the theory of general linguistics*. Amsterdam: North-Holland.

Dik, Simon. 1983. Two constraints on relators and what they can do for us. In Simon Dik (ed.), *Advances in functional grammar*, 267–298. Dordrecht: Foris.

Dikken, Marcel den. 2006. *Relators and linkers*. Cambridge, MA: MIT Press.

Den Dikken, Marcel. 2018. *Dependency and directionality*. Cambridge University Press.

Dougherty, Ray C. 1970. A grammar of coordinate conjoined structures: I. *Language* 46.4: 850–898.

Embick, David and Rolf Noyer. 2001. Movement operations after syntax. *Linguistic Inquiry* 32.4: 555–595.

Embick, David and Rolf Noyer. 2012. Distributed morphology and the syntax-morphology interface. In Gillian Ramchand and Charles Reiss (eds.), *The Oxford handbook of linguistic interfaces*, 289–324. New York: Oxford University Press. DOI: 10.1093/oxfordhb/9780199247455.013.0010.

von Fintel, Kai. 2001. Counterfactuals in a dynamic context. In Michael Kenstowicz (ed.), *Ken Hale: A life in language*, 123–152. MIT Press.

Fox, Danny and Kyle Johnson. 2016. QR is restrictor sharing. *Proceedings of the 33rd West Coast Conference on Formal Linguistics*, 1–16. Somerville, MA: Cascadilla Proceedings Project.

Franco, Ludovico and Rita Manzini. 2017. Instrumental prepositions and case: Contexts of occurrence and alternations with datives. *Glossa: A Journal of General Linguistics* 2.1: 8. 1–37, DOI: https://doi.org/10.5334/gjgl.111

Franks, Steven. 1992. A prominence constraint on null operator constructions. *Lingua* 88: 1–20.

Freidin, Robert. 2020. *Adventures in English syntax*. Cambridge University Press.

Gawron, Jean Mark and Andrew Kehler. 2004. The semantics of respective readings, conjunction, and filler-gap dependencies. *Linguistics and Philosophy* 27: 169–207.

Gazdar, Gerald. 1981. Unbounded dependencies and coordinate structure. *Linguistic Inquiry* 12: 155–183.

Gehrke, Berit and Elena Castroviejo. 2015. Manner and degree: An introduction. *Natural Language & Linguistic Theory* 33.3: 745–790.

George, Leland. 1980. *Analogical generalization in natural language syntax*. Doctoral dissertation, MIT.

Georgi, Doreen and Mary Amaechi. 2020. Resumption and islandhood in Igbo. *Proceedings of the 50th Annual Meeting of the North East Linguistic Society*, 261–274. Amherst, MA: GLSA.

Gleitman, Lila. 1965. Coordinating conjunctions in English. *Language* 41.2: 260–293.

Goodall, Grant. 1987. *Parallel structures in syntax: Coordination, causatives and restructuring*. Cambridge: Cambridge University Press.

Grosu, Alexander. 1973. On the nonunitary nature of the coordinate structure constraint. *Linguistic Inquiry* 4.1: 88–92.

Grosu, Alexander. 1985. Subcategorization and parallelism. *Theoretical Linguistics* 12.2: 231–239.

Grosu, Alexander. 1987. On acceptable violations of parallelism constraints. In R. Dirven and V. Fried (eds.), *Functionalism in linguistics*, 425–457. Amsterdam: John Benjamins.

Haegeman, Liliane. 2022. Typology of adverbial clauses. Handout given at the workshop Typology of Adverbial Clauses and the Role of Discourse Syntax, Cologne, May 20–21.

Haida, Andreas and Sophie Repp. 2012. Locality restrictions on sideward movement. Manuscript. http://ling.auf.net/lingbuzz/001666.

Haspelmath, Martin. 2004. Coordinating constructions: An overview. In Martin Haspelmath (ed.), *Coordinating constructions*, 3–40. John Benjamins.

Heim, Irene and Angelika Kratzer. 1998. *Semantics in generative grammar*. Oxford: Blackwell.

Hendriks, Petra. 2004. *Either, both* and *neither* in coordinate structures. In Alice ter Meulen and Werner Abraham (eds.), *The composition of meaning: From lexeme to discourse*. Amsterdam: John Benjamins, 115–138.

Heycock, Caroline and Roberto Zamparelli. 2003. Coordinated bare definites. *Linguistic Inquiry* 34.3: 443–469.

Hockett, Charles Francis. 1958. *A course in modern linguistics*. New York: The Macmillan Company.

Hoeksema, Jack. 2000. Negative polarity items: Triggering, scope, and c-command. In Laurence R. Horn and Yasuhiko Kato (eds.), *Negation and polarity: Syntactic and semantic perspectives*, 115–146. Oxford: Oxford University Press.

Hornstein, Norbert and Jairo Nunes. 2002. On asymmetries between parasitic gap and Across-The-Board constructions. *Syntax* 5.1: 26–54.

Huang, C-T. James. 1984. Phrase structure, lexical integrity, and Chinese compounds. *Journal of the Chinese Language Teachers Association* 19.2: 53–78.

Huang, Chu-Ren. 1989. Mandarin Chinese NP de – a comparative study of current grammatical theories. Nankang, Taipei.

Huddleston, Rodney and Geoffrey Pullum. 2006. Coordination and subordination. In B. Aarts and A. McMahon (eds.), *A handbook of English linguistics*, 198–219. Blackwell.

Jackendoff, Ray. 1977. *X syntax: A study of phrase structure.* Cambridge, MA: MIT Press.

Johannessen, Janne Bondi. 1998. *Coordination.* Oxford: Oxford University Press.

Johnson, Kyle. 2018. Gapping and stripping. In Jeroen van Craenenbroeck and Tanja Temmerman (eds.), *The Oxford handbook of ellipsis*, 562–604. Oxford: Oxford University Press.

Kayne, Richard. 1994. *The antisymmetry of syntax.* Cambridge, MA: MIT Press.

Kayne, Richard. 2022. Antisymmetry and externalization. *Studies in Chinese Linguistics* 43.1: 1–20.

Kazenin, Konstantin. 2002. On coordination of *wh*-phrases in Russian. Manuscript, Tübingen University and Moscow State University.

Kehler, Andrew. 2002. *Coherence, reference, and the theory of grammar.* Stanford, CA: CSLI Publications.

Keshet, Ezra and David J. Medeiros. 2019. Imperatives under coordination. *Natural Language & Linguistic Theory* 37.3: 869–914.

Koster, Jan. 1978. Why subject sentences don't exist. In S. J. Keyser (ed.), *Recent transformational studies in European languages*, 53–64. Cambridge, MA: MIT Press.

Kučerová, Ivona and Alan Munn. 2023. Beyond φ-features: Are we there yet? Agree reconsidered. Paper presented at WECCFL-41.

Lakoff, George. 1986. Frame semantic control of the coordinate structure constraint. In Anne M. Farley, Peter T. Farley, and Karl-Erik McCullough (eds.), *Papers from the Chicago linguistic society* 22, Part 2, 152–167.

Lakoff, George and Stanley Peters. 1969. Phrasal conjunction and symmetric predicates. In David A. Reibel and Sanford A. Schane (eds.), *Modern studies in English*, 113–142. Englewood Cliffs, NJ: Prentice-Hall.

Langacker, Ronald. 1969. On pronominalization and the chain of command. In D. A. Reibel, S. A. Schane, N. Chomsky, and G. Lakoff (eds.), *Modern studies in English: Readings in transformational grammar*, 160–186. Englewood Cliffs, NJ: Prentice-Hall.

Larson, Richard K. 2018. AP-de (地) adverbs in Mandarin. *Studies in Chinese Linguistics* 39.1: 1–28.

Larson, Richard and Hiroko Yamakido. 2008. Ezafe and the deep position of nominal modifiers. In L. McNally and C. Kennedy (eds.), *Adjectives and adverbs: Syntax, semantics, and discourse*, 43–70. Oxford: Oxford University Press.

Levin, Beth 1993. *English verb classes and alternations: A preliminary investigation*. Chicago: University of Chicago Press.

Li, Yafei. 2022. *Universal grammar and iconicity*. Cambridge University Press.

Li, Y.-H. Audrey. 2008. Phrase structure and categorial labelling: *de* as a head? *Dangdai Yuyanxue* [Contemporary Linguistics] 10.2: 97–108.

Lohndal, Terje. 2014. Sentential subjects: Topics or real subjects. *Proceedings of the 31st West Coast Conference on Formal Linguistics (WCCFL 31)*, 315–324. Cascadilla, MA: Cascadilla Proceedings Project.

Marantz, Alec. 1997. No escape from syntax: Don't try morphological analysis in the privacy of your own lexicon. University of Pennsylvania. *Working Papers in Linguistics* 4.2: 201–225.

McCawley, James. 1982. Parentheticals and discontinuous constituent structure. *Linguistic Inquiry* 13.1: 91–106.

McInnerney, Andrew and Yushi Sugimoto. 2022. On dissociating adjunct island and subject island effects. *Proceedings of Linguistic Society of America* 7.1: 5207. https://doi.org/10.3765/plsa.v7i1.5207.

McKinney-Bock, Katherine. 2013. Deriving split-antecedent relative clauses. *University of Pennsylvania Working Papers in Linguistics* 19.1(14): 113–122.

McNally, Louise 1992. VP-coordination and the VP-internal subject hypothesis. *Linguistic Lnquiry* 23.2: 336–341.

Mel'čuk, Igor Aleksandrovic. 1988. *Dependency syntax: Theory and practice*. Albany, NY: The SUNY Press.

Mitrović, Moreno. 2014. *Morphosyntactic atoms of propositional logic*. Doctoral dissertation, University of Cambridge.

Mittwoch, Anita. 2005. Do states have Davidsonian arguments? Some empirical considerations. In C. Maienborn and A. Wöllstein (eds.), *Event arguments: Foundations and applications*: 69–88. Tübingen: Max Niemyer Verlag.

Moltmann, Friederike. 1992. *Coordination and comparatives*. Doctoral dissertation, MIT (e-version).

Moltmann, Friederike. 2004. The semantics of *together*. *Natural Language Semantics* 12.4: 289–318.

Mouret, François. 2004. The syntax of French conjunction doubling. *Proceedings from the annual meeting of the Chicago Linguistic Society*. 40.2: 193–207.

Muadz, Husni. 1991. *Coordinate structure: A planar representation*. Doctoral dissertation, University of Arizona.

Munn, Alan 1987. Coordinate structure and X-bar theory. *McGill Working Papers in Linguistics* 4.1: 121–140.

Munn, Alan. 1992. A null operator analysis of ATB gaps. *The Linguistic Review* 9: 1–26.

Munn, Alan. 1993. *Topics in the syntax and semantics of coordinate structures*. Doctoral dissertation, University of Maryland, College Park.

Munn, Alan. 1999. On the identity requirement of ATB extraction, *Natural Language Semantics* 7.4: 421–425.

Munn, Alan. 2000. Three types of coordination asymmetries. In Kerstin Schwabe and Ning Zhang (eds.), *Ellipsis in conjunction*, 1–22. Niemeyer.

Neeleman, Ad, Joy Philip, Misako Tanaka, and Hans van de Koot. 2023. Subordination and binary branching. *Syntax* 26.1: 41–84.

Nichols, Johanna. 1986. Head-marking and dependent-marking grammar. *Language* 62.1: 56–119.

Nunes, Jairo. 2001. Sideward movement. *Linguistic Inquiry* 32: 303–344.

Oda, Hiromune. 2017. Two types of the coordinate structure constraint and rescue by PF deletion. In Andrew Lamont and Katerina Tetzloff (eds.), *Proceedings of the 47th Annual Meeting of the North East Linguistic Society*, 343–356. Amherst, University of Massachusetts, Graduate Linguistic Student Association.

Oda, Hiromune. 2021. Decomposing and deducing the coordinate structure constraint. *The Linguistic Review* 38.4: 605–644.

Özay-Demircioğlu, Ayşe Gül. 2021. Processing of Comitative Constructions in Turkish. Manuscript. TED University.

Panagiotidis, Phoevos and Vitor Nóbrega. 2023. Why we need roots in Minimalism. To appear in 2024 in *Cambridge Handbook of Minimalism*. lingbuzz/006497

Parsons, Terence. 1990. *Events in the semantics of English: A study in sub-atomic semantics*. Cambridge, MA: MIT Press.

Patejuk, Agnieszka, and Adam Przepiórkowski. 2023. Category mismatches in coordination vindicated. *Linguistic Inquiry* 54.2: 326–349.

Payne, John. 1985. Complex phrases and complex sentences. In Timothy Shopen (ed.), *Language typology and syntactic description* II, 3–41, Cambridge: Cambridge University Press.

Perlmutter, David M., and John Robert Ross. 1970. Relative clauses with split antecedents. *Linguistic Inquiry* 1.3: 350–350.

Pesetsky, David. 1991. Zero Syntax. vol. 2: Infinitives. Material intended for "Zero Syntax" but not included in the final publication. Available at http://lingphil.mit.edu/papers/pesetsk/infins.pdf, accessible on August 11, 2022.

Peterson, Peter G. 2004. Coordination: Consequences of a lexical–functional account. *Natural Language and Linguistic Theory* 22: 643–679.

Petzell, Erik M. 2017. Head conjuncts: Evidence from Old Swedish. *Linguistic Inquiry* 48.1: 129–157.

Philip, J. Naomi. 2012. *Subordinating and coordinating linkers*. Doctoral dissertation, University College London.

Pietraszko, Asia. 2019. Obligatory CP nominalization in Ndebele. *Syntax* 22.1: 66–111.

Postal, Paul Martin. 1998. *Three investigations of extraction*. MIT Press.

Prażmowska, Anna. 2013. Polish coordination as adjunction. In *Proceedings of the Second Central European Conference in Linguistics for Postgraduate Students*, 203–218.

Privoznov, Dmitry. 2021. A theory of two strong islands. MIT dissertation.

Progovac, Ljiljana. 1998. Structure for coordination. *Glot international* 3.7: 3–6.

Progovac, Ljiljana. 1999. Events and economy of coordination. *Syntax* 2.2: 141–159.

Progovac, Ljiljana. 2002. Correlative conjunctions and events: A reply to a reply. *Syntax* 5.3: 277–283.

Przepiórkowski, Adam. 2022a. Coordination of unlike grammatical cases. *Language* 98.3: 592–634.

Przepiórkowski, Adam. 2022b. Polyadic cover quantification in heterofunctional coordination. In Daniel Gutzmann and Sophie Repp (eds.), *Proceedings of Sinn und Bedeutung* 26: 677–696. University of Cologne.

Richards, Norvin. 2010. *Uttering trees*. MIT Press.

Ross, John Robert. 1967. *Constraints on variables in syntax*. Doctoral dissertation, MIT.

Rubin, Edward. 1994. *Modification: A syntactic analysis and its consequences*. Doctoral dissertation, Cornell University, Ithaca, NY.

Rubin, Edward. 2003. Determining pair-merge. *Linguistic Inquiry* 34.4: 660–668.

Safir, Ken. 2022. Just Pair-merge: Are adjuncts syntactically defined by operations or representations? Manuscript. Rutgers University.

Sag, Ivan, Gerald Gazdar, Thomas Wasow, and Steven Weisler. 1985. Coordination and how to distinguish categories. *Natural Language and Linguistic Theory* 3: 117–171.

Salzman, Martin. 2012. A derivational ellipsis approach to A TB-movement. *The Linguistic Review* 29.3: 397–438.

Salzman, Martin. 2015. Deriving mismatches in ATB-movement: Asymmetric extraction + ellipsis. Manuscript. University of Leipzig.

Schachter, Paul. 1977. Constraints on coordination. *Language* 53.1: 86–103.

Schein, Barry. 2017. *"And": Conjunction reduction redux*. MIT Press.

Shushurin, Philip. 2022. Adjectival morphology, ezafe and prepositions: Towards a new analysis of linkers. Handout in the Tel Aviv University Syntax Workshop.

Sjoblom, Todd. 1980. *Coordination*. Doctoral dissertation, MIT.

Sledd, James. 1959. *A short introduction to English grammar*. Chicago: Scott, Foresman and Co.

Stolz, Thomas, Cornelia Stolz, and Aina Urdze. 2006. *On comitatives and related categories: A typological study with special focus on the languages of Europe*. Berlin: Mouton de Gruyter.

Tai, James H.-Y. 1969. *Coordination reduction*. Doctoral dissertation, Indiana University.

Takano, Yuji. 2004. Coordination of verbs and two types of verbal inflection. *Linguistic Inquiry* 35.1: 168–178.

Tang, C.-C. Jane. 2008. Functional extension vs. grammaticalization: A typological study of modification markers in Formosan nominals. *Language and Linguistics* 9.4: 917–966.

te Velde, John. 2005. *Deriving coordinate symmetries: A phase-based approach integrating Select, Merge, Copy and Match*. Amsterdam: John Benjamins.

Thiersch, Craig. 1985. VP and scrambling in the German Mittelfeld. Manuscript, University of Tilburg.

Ting, Jen. To appear. A unified approach to parasitic gap and across-the-board constructions: Evidence based on Mandarin Chinese. *Syntax*.

Tremblay, Mireille. 1996. Lexical and non-lexical prepositions in French. In A.-M. DiSciullo (ed.), *Configurations*. Somerville, MA: Cascadilla Press.

Tsai, Wei-Tien Dylan and Chun-Ming Wu. 2012. Conjunctive reduction revisited: Evidence from Mayrinax Atayal and Southern Paiwan. *Oceanic Linguistics* 51.1: 160–181.

van Oirsouw, Robert. 1987. *The syntax of coordination*. New York: Croom Helm.

Vergnaud, Jean-Roger. 1974. *French relative clauses*. Doctoral dissertation, MIT, Cambridge, MA.

Vries, Mark de. 2005. Coordination and syntactic hierarchy. *Studia Linguistica* 59.1: 83–105.

Vries, Mark de. 2017. Across-the-Board phenomena. *The Wiley Blackwell Companion to Syntax*, Second Edition, 20–50. John Wiley & Sons.

Weisser, Philipp. 2020. How Germans move their "but"s: A case of prosodic inversion across phrases. In M. Asatryan, Y. Song, and A. Whitmal (eds.), *Proceedings of NELS 50*, online. Amherst, MA: GLSA.

Welmers, William E. 1973. *African language structures*. Berkeley: University of California Press.

Whitman, Philip Neal. 2002. *Category neutrality: A type-logical investigation*, PhD diss., The Ohio State University.

Whitman, Philip Neal. 2004. Semantics and pragmatics of English verbal dependent coordination. *Language* 80.3: 403–434.

Wilder, Chris. 1994. Coordination, ATB, and ellipsis. *Groninger Arbeiten zur germanistischen Linguistik* 37: 291–331.

Wilder, Chris. 1997. Some properties of ellipsis in coordination. In Artemis Alexiadou and T. Alan Hall (eds.), *Studies on universal grammar and typological variation*, 59–107. Amsterdam: John Benjamins.

Wilder, Chris. 1999. The syntax of coordination. Handout of Linguistic Summer School, Potsdam University.

Wilder, Chris. 2008. Shared constituents and linerarization. In Kyle Johnson (ed.), *Topics in ellipsis*, 229–258. Cambridge: Cambridge University Press.

Williams, Alexander. 2015. *Arguments in syntax and semantics*. Cambridge University Press.

Williams, Edwin. 1977. Across-the-Board application of rules. *Linguistic Inquiry* 8.2: 419–423.

Williams, Edwin. 1978. Across-the-Board rule application. *Linguistic Inquiry* 9.1: 31–43.

Williams, Edwin. 1981. Transformationless grammar. *Linguistic Inquiry* 12.4: 645–653.

Williams, Edwin. 1990. The ATB theory of parasitic gaps. *The Linguistic Review* 6: 265–279.

Winter, Yoad. 1994. Syncategorematic conjunction and structured meanings. In M. Simons and T. Galloway (eds), *Proceedings of semantics and linguistic theory (SALT)* 5, 387–404. CLC Publications, Department of Linguistics, Cornell University. Ithaca, NY.

Winter, Yoad. 2001. Flexibility principles in Boolean semantics: The interpretation of coordination, plurality, and scope in natural language. Cambridge, MA: MIT Press.

Wu, Danfeng. 2022. *Syntax and prosody of coordination*. Doctoral dissertation, MIT.

Yngve, Victor H. 1960. A model and a hypothesis for language structure. *Proceedings of the American Philosophical Society* 104: 444–466.

Zhang, Niina Ning. 2007. The syntactic derivations of split antecedent relative clause constructions. *Taiwan Journal of Linguistics* 5.1: 19–47.

Zhang, Niina Ning. 2008a. Encoding exhaustivity. *UST Working Papers in Linguistics* 4, 133–143. National Tsing Hua University.

Zhang, Niina Ning. 2008b. Repetitive and correlative coordinators as focus particles parasitic on coordinators. *SKY Journal of Linguistics* 21: 295–342.

Zhang, Niina Ning. 2010. *Coordination in syntax*. Cambridge: Cambridge University Press.

Zhang, Niina Ning. 2014. Summing quantities of objects at the left edge. *Taiwan Journal of Linguistics* 12.2: 33–58.

Zhang, Niina Ning. 2015. The morphological expression of plurality and pluractionality in Mandarin. *Lingua* 165: 1–27.

Zhang, Niina Ning. 2022. Could there be other functional elements? Workshop on Foundations of Extended Projections, Tromsø, October 27–28.

Zhu, Dexi. 1980. Beijing-hua, Guangzhou-hua, Shuiwen-hua he Fuzhou-hua li de DE zi [DE in Beijing, Guangzhou, Shuiwen, and Fuzhou dialects], *Fangyan* 1980.3: 161–165.

Zoerner, Ed. 1995. *Coordination: The syntax of andP*. Doctoral dissertation, University of California, Irvine.

Zoerner, Ed. 1999. One coordinator for all. *Linguistic Analysis* 29.3/4: 324–341.

Zorzi, Giorgia. 2018. Coordination in Catalan sign language: A syntactic account for conjunction. *FEAST* 2: 132–142.

Zwart, Jan-Wouter. 2005. Some notes on coordination in head-final languages. *Linguistics in the Netherlands* 2005: 231–242.

Zyman, Erik. 2020. In situ mixed wh-coordination and the argument/adjunct distinction. *Glossa: A Journal of General Linguistics* 5.1: 30. 1–13. DOI: https://doi.org/10.5334/gjgl.1070

Acknowledgments

Early versions of parts of this Element have benefited from comments from David Adger, Yichun Chen, Tim Chou, Michael Diercks, Jowang Lin, Asia Pietraszko, Shuying Shyu, Peter Svenonius, Dylan Tsai, Susi Wurmbrand, Barry Yang, Ching-Yu, Yang, and the rest of the audiences at the Fourteenth Workshop on Formal Syntax and Semantics (Taipei, October 21–22, 2022) and the Workshop on Foundations of Extended Projections (Tromsø, October 27–28, 2022). Special thanks go to Phoevos Panagiotidis and Edith Aldridge for their very helpful comments on early drafts. James Myers helped me with the data and Sam Wang with the references. The two anonymous reviewers gave me very detailed and valuable comments. Importantly, Robert Freidin encouraged me to return to coordination and helped me to start the project, when I thought I had no more to say after my 2010 book. He also pushed me to clarify my points again and again. I feel very lucky and grateful to him. Remaining errors are mine. This research has been partially supported by grants from the National Science and Technology Council, Taiwan.

Cambridge Elements ≡

Generative Syntax

Robert Freidin
Princeton University

Robert Freidin is Emeritus Professor of Linguistics at Princeton University. His research on syntactic theory has focused on cyclicity, case and binding, with special emphasis on the evolution of the theory from its mid-twentieth century origins and the conceptual shifts that have occurred. He is the author of *Adventures in English Syntax* (Cambridge 2020), *Syntax: Basic Concepts and Applications* (Cambridge 2012), and *Generative Grammar: Theory and its History* (Routledge 2007). He is co-editor with Howard Lasnik of *Syntax: Critical Assessments* (6 volumes) (Routledge 2006).

About the Series

Cambridge Elements in Generative Syntax presents what has been learned about natural language syntax over the past sixty-five years. It focuses on the underlying principles and processes that determine the structure of human language, including where this research may be heading in the future and what outstanding questions remain to be answered.

Cambridge Elements ≡

Generative Syntax

Elements in the Series

Merge and the Strong Minimalist Thesis
Noam Chomsky, T. Daniel Seely, Robert C. Berwick, Sandiway Fong,
M.A.C. Huybregts, Hisatsugu Kitahara, Andrew McInnerney and Yushi Sugimoto

Coordinate Structures
Ning Zhang

A full series listing is available at www.cambridge.org/EGSY

Printed in the USA
CPSIA information can be obtained
at www.ICGtesting.com
LVHW011301150324
774517LV00048B/2564